Children of the Rainforest

Rutgers Series in Childhood Studies

The Rutgers Series in Childhood Studies is dedicated to increasing our understanding of children and childhoods throughout the world, reflecting a perspective that highlights cultural dimensions of the human experience. The books in this series are intended for students, scholars, practitioners, and those who formulate policies that affect children's everyday lives and futures.

Series Board

For a list of all the titles in the series, please see the last page of the book.

Children of the Rainforest

Shaping the Future in Amazonia

CAMILLA MORELLI

With a foreword and afterword by Roldán Dunú Tumi Dësi

RUTGERS UNIVERSITY PRESS

NEW BRUNSWICK, CAMDEN, AND NEWARK, NEW JERSEY

LONDON AND OXFORD

Rutgers University Press is a department of Rutgers, The State University of New Jersey, one of the leading public research universities in the nation. By publishing worldwide, it furthers the University's mission of dedication to excellence in teaching, scholarship, research, and clinical care.

978-1-9788-2522-2 (cloth)
978-1-9788-2521-5 (paper)
978-1-9788-2523-9 (epub)
978-1-9788-2525-3 (web pdf)

Cataloging-in-publication data is available from the Library of Congress.

LCCN 2023932725

A British Cataloging-in-Publication record for this book is available from the British Library.

References to internet websites (URLs) were accurate at the time of writing. Neither the author nor Rutgers University Press is responsible for URLs that may have expired or changed since the manuscript was prepared.

♾ The paper used in this publication meets the requirements of the American National Standard for Information Sciences—Permanence of Paper for Printed Library Materials, ANSI Z39.48-1992.

rutgersuniversitypress.org

To Andrew Irving

CONTENTS

FOREWORD

My name is Roldán Dunú Tumi Dësi. I am a member of the Matses Indigenous group of the Peruvian Amazon. I speak two languages, my native tongue and Spanish. I grew up in Buenas Lomas Antigua, a small community that is very far from the city and surrounded by the forest.

When I finished high school, I left my community and came to the city of Iquitos to study social anthropology. One day I received a message from a Matses friend, who said he was working with a foreign anthropologist who had come from Europe. At the time I was in my third year. I was very excited when I heard that an anthropologist wanted to talk to me, and I wanted to meet her to find out about her research and the work she did in the field, and thus learn more about anthropology. That anthropologist who wanted to talk to me was Camilla. She had been working in the Matses communities for a while, mainly with children. We met in Iquitos and started working together, as we are still doing now.

Camilla is the first author to write a book about Matses children and young people. Matses childhood has been changing very much recently, and children in our communities face many challenges. In the past, Matses children did not attend formal schooling like they do now, but they had their own system of education where they learned from their parents and grandparents through practice. The boys learned to hunt with bows and arrows, and the girls learned to do the things their mothers did, such as weaving and producing handicrafts. Following contact with urban society, state-run schools have been introduced in Matses communities and now the children learn to read, write, and study math in their own villages in the forest, but they no longer learn about traditional ways of living. They hardly go hunting anymore, and they like to do other things instead, like play football, volleyball, and other games.

Matses people live deep inside the Amazon forest, however, and it is difficult for the national authorities and outsiders to know the reality or problems that exist in our communities. This book can hopefully allow outsiders to find out about the needs, experiences, and worldviews of Matses children and youth, so that more people beyond our own communities can learn about them.

A book on Matses children and youth is important so they can be known not just by people from outside, but especially by those who want to work with

Matses children in the future and schoolteachers from the city who come to teach in our communities. The ways children live and grow up in Matses society is different from other places, and I believe it's important before entering a community to know how the children there live, and what their own customs are. I hope that people in the city and outside our communities will at least get to know the Matses through the book, even though they have never met directly.

ROLDÁN DUNÚ TUMI DËSI IS AN Indigenous Amazonian anthropologist. He obtained a degree in anthropology at the Universidad Nacional de la Amazonía Peruana (UNAP) in Iquitos, Peru.

Children of the Rainforest

Introduction

I think the reason that boredom is the principal affliction of school children
in the United States . . . is that they are bored with the artificial world.
The artificial world *is* boring.

—Margaret Mead (1977, 22; emphasis in original)

Concrete is great. I love concrete.

—Paloma, six-year-old Matses girl

Iquitos is a large city built in the middle of the Amazon rainforest, in northern
Peru. Paloma, a six-year-old Matses girl, offers a dramatic representation of the
city's bustling center and grand architecture in a drawing (figure 1). Her image
conveys a vivid sense of life in the urban landscape, where huge tarmac streets
zigzag across the city and black houses made of concrete are connected by
power lines to the electrical grid. Gigantic lampposts tower over the houses and
shed light over everything, while beneath them bubble-shaped cars carry passengers along Iquitos's busy streets. The car in the very center of the drawing
contains two people: Paloma and her mother, who are driving around and
observing all that urban life has to offer.

And yet Paloma has never been to a city, seen a tarmac street, or traveled in
a car. She is growing up in a village set fairly deep in the Amazon rainforest, and
from there it takes at least eight hours in a canoe and then an additional one-
hour flight to reach Iquitos. Despite this wide geographical distance, the urban
world is of paramount concern in the everyday imagination, play, and speech of
Paloma and her peers, as Paloma voices herself when she says *cemento bunqui-
oebi*, which translates as "I love concrete" or more accurately "I *crave* concrete."

1

FIGURE 1 Iquitos (drawing by Paloma, six years old).

Contrary to Margaret Mead's statement quoted above, for these rainforest children the artificial world of concrete is not boring at all but captivating and intriguing, and from an early age they begin craving urban affordances that are not available in their villages.

This book explores the experiences, lived and imagined, of children and young people growing up in a time of radical shifts and readjustments in Amazonia. It draws on ethnographic fieldwork that I have been conducting with the Matses, a group of forest dwellers who have lived in voluntary isolation until fairly recently. Having worked with them for the past decade, returning every year to their villages in the rainforest, I have closely followed the life trajectories of the children, watching them grow into new kinds of persons compared with the generations before them. In this book I trace the children's journeys toward uncharted horizons, and in the process propose an ethnographic theory of social change and the future of Amazonia grounded in children's own perspectives.

When Forest Spirits Wear Sunglasses: A Child-Centered Theory of Social Change in Amazonia

The Matses comprise between two and three thousand individuals settled in a contiguous territory in northwest Amazonia, on the borders of Peru and Brazil.

The whole population lived nomadically in small groups scattered throughout the forest until the end of the 1960s, when they were approached by evangelical missionaries; prior to this, they relied solely on the use of natural resources and had only violent exchanges with other groups of people. Following missionary contact, they began to establish sedentary villages closer to navigable watercourses and the land of *chotac*, a word that translates as "non-Indigenous people," but right up to the 1990s the group had barely any direct interactions with the world beyond their own communities.

The few decades after missionary contact have seen decreases in or outright rejection of many traditional practices such as warfare, polygyny, chanting, myth telling, and initiation rites, and the simultaneous spread of new activities influenced by *chotac* people and government policies. These include the introduction of state-run schools in their communities, a gradual replacement of medicinal plants with pharmaceuticals, and increasing consumption of imported food such as rice and salt, among others. The Matses also started using an array of manufactured goods such as axes, machetes, fishing tools, clothes, and shotguns that can only be purchased in *chotac* settlements. So while their villages remain fairly remote in the forest and their daily subsistence is still largely based on hunting, fishing, horticulture, and the use of natural resources available in their surroundings, they are becoming increasingly dependent on trading bonds and exchanges with outsiders.[1]

There are nevertheless crucial disparities in how different generations of Matses are responding to the growing influences of *chotac* people and the national society. The older generations—especially those born before or during the 1970s and early 1980s—have spent their childhood and teenage years in the forest, and to this day, they continue to practice many of the traditional activities they learned in their youth and to nurture a close practical and affective relationship with the forest environment. They trek and hunt regularly, know how to forage wild foods, and collect and use medicinal plants, and they can handcraft a variety of objects like hammocks and bows and arrows.

The current generations of children and teenagers were instead born at a time when contact with the outside was already established, and they are becoming increasingly distanced from the forest-based lifestyles of their elders. Indeed, my original goal when I started carrying out research with them, over ten years ago, was to examine the children's relationship with the forest environment and its inhabitants. I had never been to Matses villages before the start of my fieldwork, and in my own imagination I pictured the children playing in and talking about the forest all day long, assuming that it would be the foundation of their imaginative and practical lives.

But the children made clear from the start that they had little if any desire to talk about the forest. Whenever I asked them about animals, hunting, or spirits, they would shrug and say, "Go and ask my grandparents about the forest,"

FIGURE 2 A *mayan* that spins
in the air (drawing by Bridget,
three years old).

and they kept bringing our conversations back around to the world of urban
people, manufactured objects, and television. They rarely mentioned the forest
spontaneously and never with the same enthusiasm and passion shown by their
elders, and they barely ever accompanied the adults on hunting treks, although
the elderly recalled doing so when they themselves were children.

Matses children were far more interested in the manufactured goods and
equipment I had brought with me, especially my camera and laptop, and would
much rather listen to me telling stories about my homeland than answer my questions about theirs, expressing their passion for the *chotac* world through both
words and images. Shortly after arriving in the village, wanting to learn about their
forest knowledge, I would often hand out blank pieces of paper and colored pencils
to the children and ask them to draw *mayan* or "spirits," which the elders often talk
about and describe as shape-shifting, malevolent creatures that mostly dwell on or
inside forest trees.

Bridget, a three-year-old girl, once drew a *mayan* that "comes forward spin-
ning around in the air, like a character I saw in a movie in town," as she described
it (figure 2). And on a different occasion, ten-year-old Simón drew a spirit that
stands on a tree branch, matching the descriptions of *mayan* he has often heard
from the elders, but this spirit is a little unusual: he has the body of a skeleton,
like the one Simón saw in a schoolbook, and wears sunglasses—perhaps the
commodity most coveted by Matses children, but rare and difficult to obtain
(figure 3).

FIGURE 3 A *mayan* that wears sunglasses (drawing by Simón, ten years old).

From our very first interactions, the children started steering the focus of our conversations out of the forest world cherished by the older generations and into an imaginative terrain crisscrossed by concrete paving, lit by the glow of electric lights and television screens, and centered around the practices and possessions of the *chotac*. A decade ago, in my first years of fieldwork, this world remained almost entirely out of reach. Most children had never even been to the city and had limited if any contact with outsiders; and if they wanted to walk on concrete pavements and watch television, they had to do so through their own imagination. They would draw themselves walking on concrete and driving in cars, like Paloma; they would spend much time describing to each other scenes from the few movies they had watched on their sporadic visits to *chotac* settlements; and the younger ones would sit on logs and pretend to be driving a motorized canoe to town to buy bread and rice (one of their favorite pretend-games).

But throughout the years, I have seen the children grow up and make tangible efforts to access that coveted elsewhere beyond their communities, striving to turn their childhood fantasies into reality—and often paying a high price for it. In the past five years or so, a growing number of teenagers and young adults have started leaving the forest and moving to nearby towns and cities, where in the attempt to satisfy their craving for concrete, they dwell in local slums and face a range of unprecedented challenges, from economic hardship to social exclusion and emotional struggles.

This phenomenon concerns not just the Matses but many other hunter-gatherer and rural populations in Amazonia and across the world, who are becoming increasingly connected to national and global circuits of trade and consumption but find themselves at their fringes (Penfield 2023; Reyes-García and Pyhälä 2017). My argument in this book is that children are not merely caught up in wider processes of change—such as large-scale urbanization, the transition to market economies, or the rise of poverty and slum dwelling across Latin America and beyond—but actively driving them, insofar as they are making choices that imply a purposeful shift away from the lifestyles and worldviews of their elders and toward new horizons.

To claim that children are agents of large-scale transformations is not to say they have direct access to political power or can make decisions for or on behalf of adults. For one thing, Matses children have no official role in the political organization of the wider community, and do not even have direct physical access to many of the things that most concern them and that they see as tangible goals for their adulthoods. For instance, they place a high value on manufactured goods, which are produced in the city and thus hard for them to access; their daily play and talk revolve around objects they have only ever seen on television, which in turn they can watch only rarely, because there is no electricity in the village; and they fantasize about the marvels of urban life although most of them have never even been to a city.

Despite these practical limitations, I argue that simply by developing their own ways of perceiving, desiring, and imagining the world, the children are becoming emotionally and affectively attached to some parts of it while turning away from others; and because this implies a shift away from the moral and affective values of the older generations, these changing desires and perceptions are creating the conditions for radically new futures. For example, when Matses children imagine the faraway world of cities and *chotac* people, they largely do so through modalities of fascination, excitement, and craving, and this very act of imagining and placing value upon it means they learn to see the urban world as an all-consuming target for their future adulthoods. By contrast, coming to know and understand the forest through feelings of boredom, fear, and fatigue means the children purposefully reject forest-based practices and distance themselves from the forest, with crucial implications for their society and its relationship with the natural environment.

Accordingly, children's desires and imaginations are powerful catalysts for social and economic change, and driving major transformations that are affecting their society and other populations in Amazonia and beyond. In order to understand how these global processes unfold, it is therefore necessary to look closely at

FIGURE 4 Edgar photographs a plantain tree (photograph by Diego, twelve years old).

the everyday and subtle contexts of play, peer group interactions, and imaginative activities through which children are developing new meanings and values.

A View from the Ground

Figure 4 shows ten-year-old Edgar holding a camera and pointing it upward, to photograph a plantain tree in his family's cultivated field. The picture was taken by Diego, twelve years old, using another of the digital cameras that I gave out to children during my fieldwork. The boys were born in the same village as Paloma, and like her, they had never been to a city or traveled outside of Amazonia at the time these photographs were taken.

Edgar's viewpoint from the ground up, pointing the camera to the forest trees above him, evokes the opening passage of *Marriage among the Trio* by Peter Rivière, one of the most influential authors in the anthropology of Amazonia:

During my months among the Trio, my world had shrunk to the size of their world. As the aeroplane lifted above the trees, the visual realization of the immensity of the Universe was thrust violently back into my awareness. It was like the reawakening of a long forgotten taste. . . . Could an Indian's eyes and mind have adjusted themselves to comprehend such a vast and undifferentiated view as the jungle affords from the air? (1969: vii).

As he looks down from the airplane, Rivière compares his airborne view from above to that of the people on the ground below. Having emerged from his fieldwork in the forest, he questions whether the eyes of someone who has spent their whole lives down there—like Paloma, Edgar, and Diego—could ever adjust to, and indeed comprehend, the change of perspective and awareness afforded by the elevated view on the airplane. It is implied, in a sense, that viewing from above generates new ways of knowing and grasping the world, where unequal technological and economic relations transform into uneven vantage positions.

Anthropologists have long critiqued this bird's-eye view as characteristic of particular anthropological approaches and power relations, first and foremost structuralism. The structuralist paradigm has been much challenged precisely for its tendency to observe people's lives as if viewed "from above," reducing thought and behavior to abstract models and structures rather than asking how people directly experience, perceive, and understand the world (Bourdieu in Bloch 2012: 149; Fabian 1983: 52–69; Salmond 1982: 74–75). And it is perhaps not much of a coincidence, therefore, that Rivière's opening account of looking down from the airplane is followed by a classic structuralist analysis of Trio marriage rules, which is focused more on the structure of social organization seen from an outside perspective than on people's lived experiences and own viewpoints.

The work of Peter Rivière was written more than half a century ago, and this is not to deny the invaluable contributions and insights offered by his work and other structuralist theories (some of which I will use in this book, to shed light on how children understand and radically change the world). But the bird's-eye view in this opening passage is somewhat emblematic of a certain kind of ethnographic gaze that has had long-lasting influence in the anthropology of Amazonia, where the focus on local systems of thought has been prioritized (and in many ways, continues to be so) over an attention to how these worldviews transform through time. Ethnographers have written a plethora of works on Amazonian worldviews, cosmologies, and "ontologies"—defined as cultural-specific ways of understanding and classifying the nature of being—and in most cases, they have presented these as abiding worldviews shared enduringly between the generations instead as changing throughout them.

This lack of attention to change is partly because the vast majority of works conducted with rural and hunter-gatherer people in Amazonia (and elsewhere across the world) have systematically disregarded children and their process of learning. While stressing the relevance of exploring people's own perspectives and viewpoints in hunter-gatherer and Indigenous societies, ethnographers have taken for granted that such views should be those of the adults, paying little if any notice to what children and youth have to say. And all across the social sciences, works that focus on children's own knowledge and voices are largely confined to Western and industrialized childhoods, while far less has been written about the worldviews and peer cultures of children in hunter-gatherer and forest-dwelling societies (Bird-David 2005; Corsaro 2011: 308). For the most part, Amazonian and hunter-gatherer children continue to be addressed from an adult-centric or bird's-eye view from above, instead of being actively engaged in the process of knowledge production as primary research respondents.

This is a relevant omission, not least because children and youth constitute the largest demographics of most Indigenous and hunter-gatherer populations across the world.[2] It is estimated that nearly half of all Amazonians in Peru are under fifteen years of age, and in the specific district where I conducted my research, 55 percent of the population is under eighteen (INEI 2007; World Bank Group 2015: 30). Ignoring the viewpoints of children and youth in these contexts means not only overlooking the actual majority of the population but also disregarding the current and future worlds these young generations are actively building. If children are the future in the making (Cohn 2014; Cole and Durham 2008) and are "actively involved in the construction of their own social lives, the lives of those around them and of the societies in which they live" (James and Prout 1997: 4), then the paucity of research carried out with Indigenous and hunter-gatherer children means their role as agents of change and future-makers has gone largely underexamined—with limited attention paid to how younger generations learn, transform, or perhaps reject the knowledge of their elders, creating a world that will be radically different from the one their parents and grandparents have built.

My foremost aim here is to move away from this adult-centric bird's-eye view by taking an approach that positions children "as participating subjects rather than as the objects of adult research" (James 2007: 262). One of my uppermost inspirations in this is the pioneering work of Margaret Mead, the first anthropologist to have taken children seriously as capable research participants. Conducting fieldwork around one hundred years ago, Mead took a groundbreaking approach by not simply observing children from a detached standpoint, but rather asking them questions and thereby recognizing them as agents who can produce meaningful knowledge independently from adults (1932, 2001 [1928]).

Mead's approach remained long unparalleled in childhood and youth studies, a field that for most of its history has been dominated by theories of socialization (i.e., works that focused on how children are raised to be competent social actors and that were built primarily on data collected by observing children and talking with adults about them). With the so-called child-centered turn in the 1980s–1990s (Montgomery 2009: 43), a number of scholars started engaging children as research participants in their own right and recognizing their ability to develop original knowledge and worldviews. Allison James was a leading scholar in this groundbreaking framework, stressing the need for researchers to listen to children's own voices and view them as autonomous meaning-makers (1998, 2007)—a notion that is now widely agreed upon in studies of childhood and youth, where this child-centered approach has become prevalent.

Child-centered works are nevertheless coming under scrutiny, for despite offering detailed accounts of children's daily interactions, play, and peer group activities, they have often failed to place these findings within a broader analysis of society beyond children's immediate day-to-day lives. The result has been a portrayal of children's worlds as though they were separate from those of adults and detached from the wider political and economic context that children inhabit. Accordingly, the overall argument that children can and do effect social change has not been sustained through in-depth and detailed ethnographic case studies offering evidence as to how children actually do this (see Lancy 2012b for an example of such a critique).

The research presented in this book is quintessentially child-centered, insofar as I address children as primary research respondents, but I also seek to move beyond this paradigm. Following Christina Toren—one of very first scholars to propose a theory of socialization that recognized children's agency within it—I examine how children "actively constitute a world that is at once the same as, and different from, the world their elders know" (1993: 463). Of late, a number of authors have developed this view further by offering rich ethnographic accounts that take seriously children's perspectives and agency, but then situate children's lives within an analysis of wider socioeconomic and political contexts. Examples of this are the work of Olga Ulturgasheva (2012) with Eveny children in Siberia; Lauren Heidbrink's (2020) ethnography of Indigenous youth from Guatemala and Mexico who have migrated to the United States; Bambi Chapin's (2014) analysis of childhood in rural Sri Lanka; and Marjorie Orellana's (2009) study of children in immigrant communities in the United States, to mention a few.

My analysis engages with this growing body of work through a focus on Amazonian childhood that frames children's everyday imagination and desires within the environmental, political, and economic constraints that these children must negotiate on a daily basis. I thereby demonstrate ethnographically how children are able to transform their society in the face of formidable material constraints, while also taking into account the ethical challenges that emerge when conducting child-centered research with Indigenous children and youth.

The Drawing House: Ethics and Collaboration
with Amazonian Children

During one of my most recent visits to the village, I shared part of the journey with a Peruvian man who was running for mayor of the Yaquerana district, which

Matses territory is formally a part of. We boarded the same eighteen-seat military aircraft in Iquitos and flew to Colonia Angamos, the closest town to Matses communities and the district's seat. And when the plane landed on the town's earthy airstrip, built in the middle of thick forest trees, a cheering crowd was awaiting the mayoral candidate. They held flags with his campaign photograph and chanted his name—a service he paid for, as I learned later, in an attempt to display his popularity and gain votes. Next to this cheering crowd stood a smaller, quieter one: that of Matses children, who heard I were also arriving on that flight (for the first time not on my own, but with a professional animator who would teach them how to make animated films) and walked all the way on the one-mile road from the town to the airstrip to meet us.

The children waited for us to unload our bags and equipment, insisting on carrying some of it, and walked back with us to the center of town. As soon as we started walking, Daisy, a ten-year-old girl from the village where I've done most of my fieldwork, asked me, "When do we play?" "I don't know, Daisy, I'm pretty exhausted so perhaps need to rest for a bit," I replied. "How long do you need to rest for?" "Just a little bit. Then we can play." "Okay. You mean today, yes?" So after a very quick hammock break, we spent the rest of the day, and the following month, drawing and making stop-motion animations together.

Matses children have welcomed me with this enthusiasm from the very start, and throughout the years I have developed close relationships of trust and deep affection with them and their parents. Becoming friendly with the adults took a while, since when I started living with the Matses I didn't speak their language (also called "Matses" and classified under the Panoan linguistic family), and at the time less than a handful of people in the village where I stayed could speak Spanish.[3] The children, instead, started interacting with me from my very first day in the village, when a crowd of them came looking for me and started pointing at my camera. They managed to explain that they wanted me to go around the village and take pictures and videos of them, and then look at the images on the small camera screen. One of the older boys wrapped his T-shirt around his head in imitation of a ninja character and picked up a smaller boy, while all the other children stood around them, highly amused by the performance taking place.

The bigger boy put his hand on the small boy's throat and moved his finger from one side to the other, screaming, "*titeiquin!*" which later on I learned to mean "I'll slit your throat!" He then whispered something in the small boy's ear, and to an explosion of laughter from all other children, the small boy stuck his tongue out of his mouth, pretending to have been killed (figure 5). When I asked, in Spanish, what they were doing, all the children screamed out laughing, "*Vandán, Vandán!*" which I eventually understood to be the name of Belgian movie star Jean-Claude Van Damme: they were reproducing an action scene they had seen on television in town.

FIGURE 5 Children enact a scene from a Jean-Claude Van Damme movie (still from a video taken by the author).

Since then, the children kept coming to look for me every day, asking to play or take photographs or wanting to draw pictures using the stationery materials that I always bring with me from the city. During my first couple of years of field-work, we would draw in a small wooden hut that the adults had built for me in the village. The children themselves named it *dibujon shubu*, the "drawing house," and this became a foundational space of interaction where we built a relation-ship of mutual trust and understanding that continues to this day.

Researchers of childhood regularly use visual techniques to engage their young participants in the research process, recognizing that children have dif-ferent attention spans and modes of expression compared with adults and may not respond well to standard techniques such as interviews, focus groups, or questionnaires (see Denov et al. 2012; Guerrero and Tinkler 2010; Thomson 2008). The use of participatory visual methods has also been much praised for enabling children "to express their everyday experiences in various self-directed and creative ways" (Kullman 2012: 3) and to determine the subjects discussed, rather than being guided by the preferences of the researcher. This was certainly the case in my own research, where visual methods allowed me to set up a form of communication with my young respondents beyond words, and to acknowledge from the start that children had a deep-seated fascination and passion for television, urban places, and *chotac* practices.

There are nevertheless key ethical challenges that emerge from conducting child-centered research based on participatory methods. As anthropologist Lisa Mitchell pointed out, the work with children is not and should never be an exchange between "equals," but instead "relationships of power, authority, and difference need to be acknowledged and integrated into the analysis" (2006: 70; see also Allerton 2016). In my research, these imbalances were heightened by my own presence not just as an adult but specifically as a European and non-Indigenous researcher working with Indigenous children and youth. Indeed, the multiple differences between the Matses and myself were often the object of our conversations in the field. Both children and adults often asked questions about our different skin color, economic status, language, and cultural backgrounds, initiating lengthy dialogues that led us to question ourselves and to learn something about each other, thereby gaining a wider understanding into the possibilities of being a person.

My aim is to take the differences between my young respondents and myself as a starting point to build what Faye Harrison called an anthropology of "dialogue and solidarity" (2010b: 101), one where radical language, cultural, and social differences can be negotiated and a common ground established. This endeavor is founded on a "genuine critical dialogue"—one where "both ethnographer and informant are able to demystify their respective understandings of themselves and the world, and arrive at some common ground" (101). In the words of anthropologist Ernesto De Martino, the ethnographic encounter is hereby understood as a dialectical mediation of such differences, aimed at "reaching that shared human ground [*quel fondo universalmente umano*] where the self and the other are encountered as two alternative possibilities for being human" (1977: 391; my translation).

In my fieldwork, the use of child-centered and participatory methodologies was foundational to achieve this shared common ground, creating what Michael Jackson called "a space of shared *inter-est*, where a plurality of people work together to create a world to which they feel they all belong" (2013: 31)—a space represented physically and symbolically by the drawing house. Faye Harrison herself pointed out that a key step toward a decolonized anthropology might be the use of experimental and inclusive methods that can go beyond text (2010a: 6), a point much echoed by visual anthropologists, who have long argued that "works of art, including images and film have long served to bring different social worlds into contact with each other" (Cox et al. 2016: 1; see also Irving 2007; Pink 2011).

As such, visual and participatory methods are not just efficient tools for data collection but can serve a political purpose, paving the way toward an inclusive anthropology founded on empathy and collaboration, where children and youth can take a dynamic role and lead the focus of the investigation. As Linda Tuhiwai

Smith put it, decolonized methodologies are crucial to recognize that "Indigenous peoples across the world have other stories to tell" (Smith 2012: 2), and a number of scholars have stressed the need for participatory approaches that can engage young participants actively in the process of knowledge production and representation (e.g., Bird-Naytowhow et al. 2017; Brant-Castellano 2004).

Here I follow these calls by taking specifically the perspective of children. Seeking a way forward for anthropology, Anand Pandian suggests that what makes the future of our discipline possible is "the aim of reinventing the world through a *shift of perspective*, the idea that the world itself can change with the assumption of another point of view" (2019: 120; emphasis added). This shift in perspective is precisely what I seek to achieve by grasping children's *view from the ground* and attempting to explore their own thoughts, understandings, and lived experiences.

Much as Rivière suggests that his view from above affords a unique vantage point onto the forest below, granting access to a realm of knowledge that could not be gained otherwise, I propose that children's unique viewpoints can significantly expand our understandings into the conditions of human life across the world and its possible future trajectories. Throughout the book, I will integrate into the text images produced by the children, mainly drawings and photographs they took with the digital cameras I distributed, to set up an analysis that takes children's views as a starting point, and from there seeks to develop an anthropological approach founded on dialogue and solidarity.

Book Structure and Outline

The primary focus of this book is on the recent and radical transformations that have taken place since the Matses were contacted by evangelical missionaries at the end of the 1960s, which have to do with Matses people's growing exchanges with the *chotac*. This is not to say that Matses society was static until contact with outsiders and only later started to change; Romanoff (1984) and Fleck (2003) have offered detailed accounts of Matses history that trace it back to at least the beginning of the twentieth century, showing how their society had been transforming before contact.

The analysis is based on field research conducted in Peruvian Amazonia, where Matses villages are formally located within the Yaquerana district, which is itself part of the department of Loreto, northern Peru (the villages settled in Brazil fall under a different political jurisdiction). I began my fieldwork in 2010 and spent twelve consecutive months with the Matses, and since then I have returned every year for two to four months. While research was conducted over the course of ten years, some of my descriptions are written in the present tense, as a way to bring to life the lived experiences of Matses children. The first six chapters of the book are based on ethnographic material I gathered between 2010 and 2015, when I worked primarily with children aged three to fifteen in the forest village, while the final chapter of the book is based on material gathered between 2016 and 2019, when I started working with the same children who have now grown up and moved to *chotac* settlements. This will place the children's lives within a longitudinal analysis, showing how they have changed over time.

To place these changes within an intergenerational perspective, chapter 1 takes the viewpoints of the children's elderly fathers and grandfathers to explore their own experiences of childhood and offer a glimpse into recent Matses history. In particular, I highlight the centrality of the forest environment for older generations of Matses, which is necessary to contextualize the children's lives in the present and to highlight how radically these have shifted away from those of their elders. In chapter 2 I use photographs taken by the children to explore their practical and affective relationships with the river environment, highlighting how their active preference for riverine livelihoods is leading to a drastic move away from the forest. Having discussed the main subsistence activities that take place in the forest and the river, in chapter 3 I explore the use of money and trade, suggesting that children are active economic agents who are actively driving a transition to market-based economies.

In chapters 4 and 5 I focus specifically on gender, exploring first the experiences of girls and young women and then those of boys, showing that children are at once reproducing the values and gendered behaviors of older generations but also radically transforming these. Chapter 6 uses children's drawings to explore how they construct the city as a place of opportunities in their everyday imagination, and in so doing learn to perceive their everyday village as lacking these opportunities, and to desire urban lifestyles for themselves in the future. Finally, chapter 7 follows the life-trajectories of some of the children I started working with in 2010, drawing on further material gathered in 2017–2019 with the same children who have now grown up and migrated to the city, where they struggle with economic hardship, discrimination, and social exclusion. As this final chapter shows, child-centered analysis can shed light on how people are drawn into globalized systems of production and consumption, and how large-scale processes unfold at the local level as a result of children's agency.

I address my respondents as *children*, but as Margaret Mead argued, "as a theoretical concept, 'the child' is a fiction" (1977: 18), meaning that childhood is itself a cultural construct, and as such must be defined according to specific historical, social, and class contexts. Here, my use of the term "childhood" translates the gender-neutral Matses term *bacuëbo*, which refers to girls and boys of between three and twelve to thirteen years of age approximately; however, much of the analysis in this book is explicitly dedicated to defining meanings and experiences of childhood that are specific to Matses society, and to highlight how these are changing through time and between generations. To ensure anonymity, I will not disclose the name of the specific village where I have conducted most of my work and all names of participants have been changed.

1

The Child in the Forest

A Glimpse into the Childhood of the Past

During my first three weeks of fieldwork in a Matses village, I spent nearly all my time with the family of Enrique, the village chief, who at the time was the only Matses person in the whole village who could speak Spanish fluently. I had never met him, but a few months prior to my fieldwork I found his contact, sent him an email, and asked if I could conduct my research there for a year. At the time, Enrique was also one of the very few Matses who could use the internet and who regularly traveled to the city, where there is electricity and connection. He quickly replied to my message, saying that I was welcome in his community, and when I arrived he hosted me in his own house. After three weeks, however, Enrique made one of his frequent trips to the city, leaving me on my own in a village where I had no other contacts, could not speak the language, and struggled to understand the basic modalities of social interaction. In the few days after his sudden departure I felt lost, alone, and worried that I would never be able to gather any meaningful knowledge or make any friends.

My experience changed drastically when an elderly couple, Julio and Serena, invited me to their house for dinner. Perhaps they took pity on me, or perhaps Enrique had instructed them to do so. After a few evenings of broken communication and laughter with his wife Serena and their teenage daughters Nancy, Tina, and Adriana, who kept pointing at different objects and asking their names in my language, finding the words hilarious ("What do you call that? F-i-r-e? Ha-ha! And that? H-a-m-m-o-c-k?! Ha-ha-ha, what kind of word is that?!") Julio told me, "You are my sister now," setting in motion a relationship of mutual obligations and deepfelt affection that continues to this day. On subsequent visits, I never failed to bring gifts and city food like rice, oil, and salt for Julio and his family, and they would make sure that I was always well fed and looked after. Serena even expressed some veiled disappointment whenever I was invited to eat with someone else—meaning that I sometimes ate two meals in a row, one with the new acquaintance and another with Julio and Serena, to the point that I gained some weight and the nickname *Camilla tsitsupa* ("big bum"), making my new family very proud. Two months after beginning my fieldwork, my life with the Matses had changed radically, and nearly every day a different family would invite me to eat and spend time with them.

During many evenings spent at Julio and Serena's house, our conversations revolved around two main topics. The girls were determined to find out absolutely everything about my homeland and my people: who my friends and family were, their names, what they did, and what they were like. Julio, meanwhile, would tell me about the world of the Matses, and as is often the case with elderly people in Amazonia and elsewhere in the world, one of his favorite subjects was stories of life *ënden* (back then), when he and Serena were themselves children and lived nomadically in the rainforest, having only limited, mainly violent contact with outsiders.

When Matses elders talk about the past or *ënden*—whether in passing remarks during the day or long tales recounted in the evening, when everyone is lying in a hammock or sitting on the wooden floor near the fire—they describe a society that was very different from the present, one where Matses people roamed the forest "wearing no clothes" and used no manufactured goods beyond a few stolen machetes. These accounts of Matses life *ënden*, when now-elderly people were themselves children, provide a valuable comparison with contemporary Matses childhood, throwing into relief the recent and ongoing changes in Matses society which are the focus of this book—first and foremost, a shift away from the world of the forest, which is no longer central to children's lives.

Stories of Childhood *Ënden*

Julio is one of the *tsësiobo* in the village, the elderly men born before missionary contact who still recall the very different kind of life Matses people led *ënden*. He claims to be in his sixties but doesn't know his exact age—calendar time was only introduced to the Matses by the missionaries, who arrived when he was already a young adult, married and with several children of his own. His wife Serena is a few years younger, but soon she will be a *macho*, an "old woman." Like Julio, she is not sure of her exact age. Julio, Serena, and their peers spent their childhoods in remote areas of the rainforest, becoming skilled trekkers, hunters, and foragers at a very young age. Until much later in life, their only contact with outsiders (the *chotac*) was the raiding in which Julio himself took part.

In these stories of childhood from the past, the *nidmëduc* or "forest" features as a vital source of nourishment, since the Matses lived primarily through hunting, and walking through the woods was a daily activity, as well as the only means of transport. The *tsësiobo* started going on long treks when they were very little, as their parents took them through the forest to collect wild fruit and berries, or to find small creeks to fish using *ancueste*, a poisonous root that brings fish to the surface in agony, making them easy to catch. The elders' bodies bear testimony to this lifelong engagement with the forest landscape: trekking every day across hard and spiky forest ground has given the elderly people thick, hard layers on the soles of their feet that are, as they say proudly, "like a shoe."

Nomadism was a crucial feature of Matses life *ënden*, as it has been for most Amazonian hunter-gatherers who have traditionally inhabited deep rainforest areas (Alexiades 2009; Rival 2002). The whole population was divided into small settlements of up to fifty individuals, who hunted every day until no more game was left in proximity to their dwellings and cultivated crops until the soil was impoverished, at which point the whole group would move, settling in a different area of the forest where game animals were still abundant and the soil fertile.

Early works in cultural ecology proposed that this kind of nomadism was a necessary adaptive response to environmental constraints. Limiting-factors theories, for example, stressed that the rainforest environment is harsh: game animals are scarce, making it hard to sustain a consistent protein income, and the soil is not rich, meaning that field crops have a short life cycle, and therefore people *have to* move continuously to find new, available resources (see Rival 2006 and Viveiros de Castro 1996 for a review). To an extent, elderly people's accounts of the past confirm these theories. Julio and Serena recount that game animals were much more abundant when they were children and that Matses people ate meat every day, and whenever animals became scarce and the soil impoverished they would move somewhere else—implying that their roaming lifestyle was indeed an adaptive strategy through which they maintained a balance with the available natural resources.

However, social anthropologists have critiqued theories of adaptation and proposed a different theoretical view, arguing that Amazonian mobility is not a mere survival strategy but an active choice driven by people's affective relationships with the forest world (Feather 2009; Rival 2002). In other words, nomadic hunter-gatherers move around not because they *need* to but because they *want* to, and specifically, because moving is a way of nurturing and maintaining a close, emotional contact with the forest environment. Indeed, while hunting and trekking have been, and continue to be, key survival strategies for Matses elders, their relationship with the forest cannot be fully understood without taking into account their affective engagement with and true passion for it, which they continue to nurture on a daily basis.

A Passion for the Forest

When I was a child, like him [points at his ten-year-old nephew] I went with my father. We attacked the *chotac*. We fired arrows at the men, and we took their machetes. We took their women, too. Young women, just like you! [points at me and laughs].

For Julio and the boys of his generation, a key part of growing up in the forest was learning how to hunt, which they did from their early years both by following their parents on hunting treks and by playing together in their peer group. The experiences of childhood, indeed the very definition of a child, are not human universals but vary widely in different cultural contexts. In many hunter-gatherer and rural societies across the world, children are seen as active and competent economic agents who are not just looked after and provided for by their parents but must take part in subsistence activities from a young age (Gaskins 2003; Lancy 2008: 76–111; Rogoff et al. 2003).

Julio and the other *tsësiobo* recall that one of their favorite games when they were children involved making small bows and arrows modeled after the big ones used by the adult men, then firing arrows at fruit on the trees to develop their marksmanship skills. As they grew older, they would start venturing into the forest around the settlements to hunt small monkeys and, as they advanced and became more capable, bigger prey such as tapirs, deer, or peccaries. Anthropologists have termed this "play work," that is, play-based activities that children perform for fun but through which they develop adult skills that are crucial for survival (Bloch and Adler, 1994; Watson-Gegeo, 2001). For example, Jean Briggs found that Inuit children learn to be fearful of large animals through play, which helps them become hunters later in life (1998: 51), and Olga Ulturga-sheva has shown that Eveny children in Siberia engage playfully with forest and animal life, until they reach a stage of adolescence marked by "the absence of play and involvement in the actual practice" (2012: 62). Likewise, by *playing* hunters with small bows and arrows, Matses boys gradually *became* hunters who could provide food and actively contribute to the family's subsistence—suggesting that play is not an inconsequential activity but a useful socialization practice linked to the subsistence economy.

Serena told me that when she was young, girls often joined the boys who went to play in the forest, taking an active role in hunting by accompanying first their brothers and then, when they were married, their husbands, and carrying home the catch. Matses people consider *bedec*, or carrying heavy loads, to be a woman's task, and this is also a task that girls became skilled at through play. In general, Matses girls went hunting and trekking less than the men, spending more of their time cultivating and harvesting crops, such as plantains or manioc (cassava). They were nevertheless very skilled forest-dwellers, and older women born before missionary contact will still walk alone in the forest to collect wild fruits or firewood, unlike later generations of young women, who never played in the forest during their own childhood and now would never trek alone, without a man or an elderly woman accompanying them.

Besides its economic goal, play-work in the forest can also be interpreted as an activity through which Julio, Serena, and their peers developed a close emotional link with their environment. As Nurit Bird-David states in her work with Nayaka people in India, hunting and gathering are not just utilitarian activities aimed at subsistence but also meaningful cosmological practices, through which hunter-gatherers come to know the forest environment "intimately, in the way one 'knows' close relatives with whom one shares intimate day-to-day life" (1992: 39). Likewise, by playing hunters and exploring the forest on their own, away from the adults, Matses children *ënden* not only became good hunters and trekkers but also developed the intimate, emotional attachment with the forest that they still show today, whereby play, developing environmental knowledge and contributing to the economy are all part of children's process of learning about the world.

This passion for the forest is still alive and clearly visible in the attitude of the elders, who always seem to brighten up when they are trekking. When we walked together, Julio was thrilled to show me the forest, astonishing me with his incredible knowledge of its inhabitants. He was able to name every plant, tree, or animal in sight and to distinguish amid the cacophony of the forest the voice of each bird, monkey, or other animal, even at a great distance, all while himself treading so softly that his prey would not hear him coming. Like all the *tsësiobo*, he is always filled with adrenaline whenever he returns from a fruitful hunt or trek, and once back in the village he will talk of nothing else for hours—his trek, the animals he saw and heard, the wild fruits he picked up— making the forest one of his favorite topics of conversation.

But this attachment does not mean that Julio and the other elders see the forest as caring for or benevolently disposed toward them. On the contrary, Matses elders talk about the *nidmëduc* as a potentially deadly place, one that poses continuous threats to its inhabitants and where the lone trekker can be taken away by a spirit, attacked by jaguars, or bitten by snakes, or can lose their way and never return home. The elders tell many stories about their encounters with *mayan*, spirits that are said to live in the forest and take various forms in order to lure humans away, as recounted by Alina, another elderly woman: "I was walking in the forest. And then suddenly I saw my brother. He said to me, 'Come with me, sister.' I started following him. He was running. I chased him. He was running very fast, and I ran fast to catch up with him. Then, he disappeared. I stopped. I realized I was lost. He wasn't my brother! He was a *mayan*."

Alina was lost and had no idea which direction she had come from. Luckily, her husband went looking for her shortly afterward, and found her deep in the forest, far from the spot where she went missing. When she told me the story, Alina said that the man was a *mayan*, a "spirit" that can assume the aspect of a person or of an animal of prey to tempt lone trekkers or hunters into the forest. For example, several men tell of hunting treks during which they started chasing a spirit disguised as a deer or a peccary who led them far from the path and then suddenly disappeared into the woods, leaving them lost and disoriented.

For elderly people, however, it is precisely this sense of peril that makes the forest thrilling and stimulating. The forest tests their skills, challenging them physically and emotionally, and learning to navigate the dangers of the wild is what helped them become *dadambo*, an adjective meaning "very manly" and which was explained to me as describing a man who is brave, strong, hardworking and skilled at hunting—which the elders still see as the defining qualities of masculinity. Everybody in the village knows about the time when Julio defended his family against a jaguar, as recounted by his wife Serena:

> We were in the forest. I had my daughter with me. She was only a baby back then; she was this big. I was young. Then we hear "Hhhhhsssss." I looked up to a tree next to us: a jaguar! "Julio, he's going to eat us! He's going to eat my baby! What are we going to do?" I was crying. I was terrified. Then Julio took a piece of wood from the ground and shook it against the jaguar. "Hhhhhssss," the jaguar kept going. Julio yelled, "Go away!" and he kept shaking the piece of wood. The jaguar ran away. Julio scared it off. He's *dadambo*, my Julio [smiles proudly].

The ability to move confidently in the dangerous forest world, learning how to trek and hunt proficiently, is what turned boys into *dadambo* men, and for Julio this also meant becoming a skilled *cuesnanquid*, a warrior who could not only take part in raiding expeditions but also protect his family from external attack. Before missionary contact, the Matses raided both other groups of Indigenous Amazonians, as well as encampments of *chotac* rubber tappers or loggers. As Julio describes these raids, the warriors would fire arrows at the men, steal goods, including tools such as machetes, and capture the young women, who were taken back to the settlements and married to their captors, spending the rest of their lives there, unlikely ever to see their families again. Although Julio did not kidnap a wife for himself, because he was too young, he remembers his older siblings doing so.

Being *dadambo* and a great hunter made Julio a desirable partner, and when he grew up, enabled him to have two wives, Ivana and Serena, and provide plenty of meat for both of them and their children. For the older generation of Matses people, one of the greatest virtues in life is being motivated and willing to *chonuadec* (work hard), something that must be developed during childhood and is quintessentially linked to the world of the forest. Despite the signs of age on his skin and his slightly stooped posture, Julio remains strong, agile, and quick and can walk for hours without slowing down, getting tired, or becoming disoriented. His world is still one of defending himself against predators like jaguars and anacondas; of forest-spirits trying to trick him and take him away to the spirit-world; of hunting tapirs, monkeys, armadillos, and other prey; and of being proud to bring back home meat to feed both his families and also, whenever I am there, his adopted sister.

Making Forest-Children

When I was a little child, my grandfather would grab me by the arm. I was scared, very scared. I tried to escape. I cried. "*Ua, ua, ua*" [mimics the sound of a crying child]. He held me and forced me to take the frog poison. Then I vomited. The poison is good. It makes children *chonuadec*. If they don't take it, children are lazy!

By his own account, when Julio was only a little child, his parents and grandparents made him take *acate*, a poisonous secretion produced by a tree frog, said to reduce laziness and instill energy, dynamism, and the motivation to *chonuadec*. I was administered *acate* on a few occasions myself, and I can testify to its frightening and painful effects—each time I fell in such a state of panic that I would always swear never to do it again.

Acate is administered as part of a ritual between an experienced, preferably elderly poison-giver and a poison-receiver, who is generally younger. The poison-giver gently burns the arm of the receiver a number of times with a burning stick, then applies the poisonous secretion to the raw, blistered skin. The more burns that are made, the more secretion one takes and, therefore, the stronger the effects of the poison. The first time I was given the poison I tried only two small burns, a laughably weak dose by Julio's standards, but the pain and fear were nevertheless overwhelming. A few seconds after receiving the poison, my heartbeat accelerated, leading to a pounding headache and sense of dizziness and disorientation. I stood up for fear of passing out, thinking that something had gone wrong and perhaps I was having an unusual allergic reaction, panicking at the thought that the closest doctor was a twelve-hour canoe journey and then a one-hour flight away. Next, my vision became blurred and everything around me turned bright, as though I were immersed in a white, blinding light. As my heart was racing and my head felt as though it was about to explode, I became nauseous and finally started vomiting—a sign that the poison's effects were coming to an end. Far from being filled with energy and dynamism, I spent the rest of the day flat out in a hammock, unable and unwilling to move.

By contrast, Julio's arms and chest are covered with the scars left of a lifelong application of the poison. As an elder himself, Julio now administers *acate* to young children in the community, from as young as three years old, with the approval and encouragement of their parents, and he mocked me for taking only two burns and being unable to move for a whole day afterward. For the Matses, it is not only morally acceptable but necessary to administer *acate* to the children—so that, unlike me, they will grow strong and tough. It is necessary to receive the poison from a competent and skilled adult, for through the ritual, the poison-giver is said to transmit something of his own personal qualities and attitudes to the poison-receiver. If someone receives the poison from Julio, this means they are likely to develop strength, courage, and a disposition to move skillfully in the forest, whereas if the poison-giver is lazy, they will pass on their laziness onto the receiver. Likewise, as the *tsësiobo* explained to me, men cannot receive the poison from women, since women are considered weaker and might pass on their weakness to the men, meaning that women can only administer the poison to other women.

A number of anthropologists have suggested that from an Amazonian perspective, what one might term the "spiritual" (including skills or moral qualities) and the "physical" (such as the materiality of the body) are not strictly separated, as in Western thought, but rather entwined (McCallum 2003; Uzendoski 2005; Viveiros de Castro 1998). As such knowledge, abilities, moral qualities, and personal attitudes, like toughness or courage, are interconnected and merged with the body. In the context of child-rearing and education, this means that adults can and must act on a child's body in order actively to stimulate the process of growth, not just physical but also moral and personal, meaning that changing a child's body also means in some sense acting on the child's personality. The few ethnographers who have examined child-rearing practices in Amazonia have indeed noticed that parents actively stimulate the development of knowledge, skills, and moral qualities in their children through physical action (Londoño-Sulkin 2001; Rival 1998; Tassinari 2007). For example, among the Cashinaua of Brazil, "experienced and successful adults are asked to massage, bathe or paint a child's body" because through "their hands they are said to pass their bodily knowledge to the child" (Lagrou 2001: 165), reinforcing a worldview in which body, knowledge, and morality are seen as developing as one.

Acate serves a similar purpose of making children grow up to be strong and hardworking. But for Julio and his generation, the poison also has the essential function of creating a connection between people and the forest, as *acate* contains *sinan*, a powerful form of energy that pervades the universe and can be transmitted between living bodies. *Sinan* is understood as a material yet invisible substance contained in some living beings, for example, the *acate* frogs and those who receive their poison, but the term can sometimes be translated as a noun meaning "marksmanship" or "will to work hard" and therefore understood as a skill, quality, or disposition, which at the same time is thought to have a physical essence. As Tobias, an old Matses man, told me, "If you have *sinan*, you catch all the animals and you never miss. People who have *sinan* work hard and never get tired. But if you don't have *sinan*, you get lazy and when you go hunting, all the animals escape. That's why we take frog poison—to get *sinan* and hunt plenty of animals."

This substance is also contained in forest beings such as tree frogs and some poisonous ants, and when assumed by persons it transmits forest-related skills and knowledge to them—suggesting a view of the universe, shared by many forest-dwelling Amazonian groups, where "the human passes into the non-human and vice versa" (Århem 1996: 185). In this view, adults must actively stimulate the passage of nonhuman substances into children's bodies to help stimulate their growth, which for Matses elders means facilitating the development of forest skills and knowledge in children by transmitting *sinan* into their bodies. *Ënden*, in the past, a few elderly men were considered exceptionally skilled at facilitating the passage of *sinan*, taking it from the forest into their own bodies and then passing it on to other (often younger) people. They took the name of *sinan menanquid*, literally "*sinan*-givers" and were known for their extraordinary courage, strength, and other *dadambo* qualities, as recounted by Leandro, another man from Julio's generation: "When I was a child, there were many *sinan menanquid* around. Now there aren't anymore. My grandfather was a *sinan menanquid*. He knew all about frog poison and the forest. When I was a child, he made me take red ant poison too. He took red ants and put them on my arm. My arm was covered with them! They bit me very hard. It was dreadful and it made me cry, but I did it. The children today don't do it anymore. They can't take it. They just can't take it."

I was once bitten by a red ant myself when I was trying to walk barefoot through the forest, and although it was only one ant, and only on my toe, I first screamed and then wept with pain, feeling shivers down my whole body. By contrast, the young Leandro would have his arm entirely covered with them when he was only a little child, because mastering pain with bravery was part of becoming *dadambo*, and wanting to prove themselves to their peers, the children were ready and willing to take the pain. The elderly people lament that today's children are much less resilient than they themselves were *ënden*, and the younger generations see *acate* mainly as a stimulant that instils dynamism and rarely if ever refer to *sinan*. Given that the development of knowledge is seen as interconnected with the body, for elderly people the children's physical inability to take the poison explains their lack of forest knowledge and skills. In this context, Leandro's nostalgic account of what could otherwise be a traumatic memory of pain is instead a testament to the closeness felt by his generation to the world of the forest.

Becoming *Matses*, Persons

In parallel to the *dadambo* men, girls were and still are encouraged to become *dayac*, meaning "hardworking." Julio's' wife Serena is petite, yet extraordinarily strong, fast, and agile. Trekking with her through the woods to and from the field where she cultivates plantains and other crops, I was in awe of the heavy loads she could carry on her head while I failed to keep up despite my tiny burden. She told me that she became *dayac* as a small child, helping her mother by cultivating the fields, cooking over the fire, transporting heavy loads of manioc and plantains on her head, and carrying out other household chores.

Around the same time she started helping her mother and becoming *dayac* herself, Serena recalls going through a rite of passage that all elders, men and women, had to undertake and that still makes them wince at the memory of its dreadful pain: receiving the traditional Matses tattoo. This consists of two black lines that encircle the mouth and cross the cheeks up to the ears for men and women and, for men only, two additional lines that bisect the sternum. Lorena, an old woman or *macho* who was born several years before missionary contact, recounts this as one of the most painful experiences of her life.

CAMILLA: How old were you when you were tattooed, Lorena?

LORENA: I was a little girl. Like this [she puts her hand out].

CAMILLA: I see. Why did you do it?

LORENA: My father convinced me. "Daughter," my father said, "the *chotac* can attack us and they'll take you away. You will be scared. If they take you, I will travel to their land and look for you. But if you are not tattooed, I will search among the faces of the *chotac* and they will all look the same, and I won't be able to spot your face among them. 'Where is my daughter?' I will say [she moves her finger back and forth in the air, scanning an imaginary crowd]. If you have the tattoo I will look at all the faces there and I'll see your tattooed face and I will say, 'There's my daughter!' And I'll take you back home with me." This is what my father said. I got scared. And I got tattooed.

CAMILLA: Was it painful?

LORENA: Yes! Dreadfully painful! Young people now don't want to be tattooed.

CAMILLA: Why is that?

LORENA: Because they want to look like the *chotac*!

Matses tattoos were made with juice produced from the fruits of *chëshëte*, the genipap tree, which from a Matses perspective is not viewed as a tree, as I am calling it here, but rather a powerful being owned by a *mayan*. As such, the *chëshëte* does not belong to the same category as papaya or plantain trees, but is instead seen as a being endowed with humanlike consciousness and intentionality. The *chëshëte* spirit is jealous of its fruits, and if it catches people picking them, will retaliate by making their children fall ill—pointing toward what might be called an animistic cosmology, that is, a particular kind of classificatory system where social relationships are seen as extending into the nonhuman world

(Bird-David 1990; Descola 1992, 1994). Philippe Descola has defined animistic cos-mologies as cultural worldviews in which living beings that across the West are seen as nonhuman, such as plants and animals, are "attributed with cul-ture" and seen as possessing "their own spiritual principles," meaning that "it is therefore possible for humans to establish with these entities personal relations of a certain kind" (1992: 114).

In Matses people's animistic worldview, the *chëshëte* spirit is indeed under-stood and treated as a being with humanlike intentionality, and having to nego-tiate this social interaction with the *chëshëte* spirit to obtain the ink indicates that tattooing, like taking frog poison, is also part of a network of reciprocal exchanges with the nonhuman world of the forest. As Lorena recounts, for her generation the tattoo was a statement of their difference from other people; of being uniquely *matses*, a term that literally means "person." While the term can be used as an ethnonym, as in the sentence "The Matses are better at hunting than the *chotac*" or "This book is about the Matses," the term is also a noun meaning "person" or "people," and is still used as such, for example, in the expression "There are plenty of *matses* there" to describe a crowded place. So, in a sense, receiving the face tattoo was a necessary rite of passage that made a child *matses*, that is, that turned them into persons.[1]

This is not to say that the Matses consider only themselves as humans and all other people as belonging to another category of being, rather that there is certainly a well-established understanding among the elders as to what are the proper ways of being a person, or in the words of Kenneth Kensinger, of "how real people ought to live" (1995). For elderly Matses, this means being a strong and brave *dadambo* man or a hardworking *dayac* woman. As Cecilia McCallum puts it (2003: 5), "in Amazonia, persons are made," which here means that being *matses* is not a condition bestowed from birth, but something that must be devel-oped as part of growing up, and that "the growth of a child is not a spontaneous process but one that requires intentional action" (Peluso 2015: 50). For the Mat-ses, the tattooing of the body was foundational to developing *matses*-ness, mean-ing, quite literally, "becoming people." This is also indicated by the fact that when non-Matses women were captured through raiding and taken back to the community as captive wives, they immediately received the tattoo so as to become part of the group.

For the elders born before contact, *chotac* people are somehow less desirable kinds of persons, both physically and in terms of their skills and abilities—or lack thereof. The term *chotac* refers principally to non-Indigenous Peruvians (*mesti-zos* in Spanish) but sometimes includes the *matses ushu*, "white people" such as myself. Both groups are mocked by the elders for being extremely lazy, fat, unable to hunt or trek, and all in all rather useless. As a *chido ushu*, a "white woman," I was myself considered by the elders as lacking many fundamental female quali-ties and skills. While I was (and still am) very close to some of the elders and, with time, we became very fond of each other, they never showed the same level of admiration, interest, or fascination as the children and young people. They mocked me for being clumsy, lazy, and only good at writing things on my laptop. I once offered to help with burning a cleared area in the forest to plant a field, which Matses families do once a year in the dry season, taking turns to help one another. We started before sunrise, and by the time the sun was out, with fire on all sides and not one inch of shade from the Amazonian heat, I had never been so worn out and craving an ice-cold shower in my life. As I sat on the stinging ground covered in sweat and mosquito bites, dehydrated, exhausted, and very much regretting having offered my help, which had turned out to be of no use anyway, except as a butt for the jokes of the elders, Leandro walked by. He had been the first to get there, and even after hours of work without a break he was still the most active and energetic of the whole group. As he saw me panting and red-faced, he grinned and shouted, "This isn't a laptop, Camilla, is it? It's a field!" and trotted back to work, amused and laughing at my incompetence.

The young generations do not share this attitude with their elders. For them, owning a laptop and being able to use it is a subject of interest and a sign of prestige, and, as Lorena complains, they "want to be just like the *chotac*." The reasons for this intergenerational difference can be traced back to the history of missionary contact, which introduced radical changes into the life of the Matses.

The Coming of the *Señoritas*

The *tsësiobo* recall the period immediately preceding missionary contact as introducing new kinds of struggles. During the 1960s, the frequency and intensity of warfare between Matses people and outsiders had increased significantly. Matses people raided the *chotac* and were themselves targeted, to the point of engaging in a real war against the Peruvian military. While the intervention was framed as a response to Matses attacks on civilians, the Peruvian government was also looking to secure new transport routes through the forest for the extraction of natural resources (Romanoff 1984: 43; see also Chirif 2017). A military expedition was organized into Matses territory, culminating in army troops invading the forest and the Peruvian air force bombing Matses settlements. While no Matses people died, the attacks caused severe anxiety, pushing many Matses families to hide deeper in the forest or relocate to neighboring areas in Brazil. Their settlements had to be moved swiftly for fear of attacks, which was tiring and made it difficult to practice horticulture for subsistence, since the fields had to be quickly abandoned. Further, the captive women brought in new diseases that couldn't be cured with medicinal plants, leading to a rising death toll. The situation reached a turning point at the end of the 1960s, when two missionary women from the Summer Institute of Linguistics approached the Matses and succeeded in establishing contact of a nonviolent kind. The Matses called them *las señoritas* (the young ladies), and recall them with much respect and affection.

The *señoritas* approached the Matses by flying over their forest settlements with a small airplane, from which they dropped objects including knives, machetes, axes, and even a radio, something Matses people had never seen and which they broke into pieces, using its wires to craft bracelets. As they flew over the Matses settlements, the *señoritas* spoke with a megaphone about Jesus, the Bible, and *Nuquinpa*, "Our Father," in perfect Matses language, which, according to Steven Romanoff, they had learned from "a Spanish-speaking captive woman who had fled her Matses captors" (1984: 50). Isaías, who is now the oldest man in the village, had heard about Jesus from his mother, herself a *chotac* Christian woman taken captive by the Matses, and he now recounts that when he heard their message, he "knew the women were good." After a few weeks, the *señoritas* built a hut in the rainforest and a group of Matses men approached them peacefully. This was August 1969, which to this date all Matses communities celebrate as *contacto Matses*, the year of Matses contact.

When I asked the elders why they welcomed the missionary women so eagerly and peacefully, the answers were always the same: firstly, they offered protection from further attacks and guaranteed peace; secondly, they provided pharmaceuticals that cured the illnesses the Matses had started catching (the two women were also trained paramedics); and finally, but perhaps most importantly, they brought in tools and manufactured goods of outstanding quality. "In the past we used our hands to plant manioc. Do you know how hard that is?" said Lorena. "We used to steal machetes from the *chotac*," said Julio, "but theirs were old, and very bad. Those of the *señoritas* were new and great."

Along with the machetes and pharmaceuticals, the *señoritas* brought with them a set of conditions: they asked the Matses to drop warfare altogether; to convert to evangelism and read the Bible, which they translated into Matses language; and to abandon most of the traditional practices that the missionaries considered profane or blasphemous, such as plant medicine and traditional chanting (some of which the Matses continued to practice behind their backs). Matses people now consider themselves Christians, although these new religious beliefs have often been merged with already well-established cosmological understandings. For example, the idea of Satan has become associated with that of the *mayan*, so that Matses people often say "there are many *Satans* in the forest," and they describe the whale or big fish from the biblical tale of Jonah in the same way they describe river dolphins, that is, as a malicious water-spirit that assumes human shape at night and looks for young persons to kidnap and take away to its underwater world.

The missionary women helped the Matses establish their first sedentary community, *Buenas Lomas*, in proximity to the Chobayaco creek, a navigable body of water, and various groups of Matses gradually abandoned their nomadic settlements and joined the community, until the whole population had been contacted. Within a very short span of time, the Matses way of life changed radically, leading to significant intergenerational differences.

Heading to the Big Water

When they lived in the deep rainforest, the Matses would always set their temporary dwellings near small creeks, which they used to access water, and also to fish using the poisonous root *ancueste*. But they purposefully dwelled away from navigable rivers for fear of the *chotac* who lived nearby and with whom they were at war. One of the major changes that followed missionary contact was the gradual transition from the forest toward wider rivers, or *acte dapa* as Matses people called them—the "big water."

The first sedentary villages established after missionary contact were still located in the inland forest (as shown on the map in figure 6), and the

FIGURE 6 Matses migration from forest villages toward navigable rivers.

missionaries created an airstrip nearby in order to reach them. In the years that followed, Matses people founded new villages, moving ever closer to wider watercourses. Whereas initially these were built farther upriver and along smaller creeks (i.e., farther south on the map), with time the Matses started moving downriver and settling on the banks of the much wider Yaquerana River and Javari River (i.e., toward the north of the map), in closer proximity to the town, Colonia Angamos, and farther away from the inland forest. A few families have established a small permanent community right on the outskirts of Colonia Angamos, named Fray Pedro, whereas other Matses people only spend short periods of time there.

This movement downriver is indicative of the extent to which, in the past few decades, the Matses have become reliant on the river as a source of nourishment and transportation, as well as on exchanges with *chotac* people and places that can only be reached by water. Matses children are growing up in a world very different from the one in which the elders spent their childhoods and where the river, town, and *chotac* are not absent or peripheral, as they were *ënden*, but rather present and even central to the economic and social life of the community.

While Matses elders continue to nurture a close relationship with the forest environment and the world of *sinan* and forest spirits, the children are increasingly distanced from it, and while to an extent reproducing the way of life of their parents and grandparents, they are also becoming dissatisfied with many aspects of it. These changes are occurring within the span of a single generation: Matses people continue to have children until late in life, meaning that many of the elders who grew up before contact in nomadic dwellings now themselves have very young children or even babies who are growing up amid radical transformations. The rest of this book will focus on this changing world, and on the ways Matses children have found of living in it.

2

River Horizons

Moving toward the Big Water

The photographs in figure 7 show children as young as three years old playing on the riverbank, swimming in the river, and paddling on canoes, activities that have become part of Matses people's daily practice. After establishing settlements on the banks of navigable watercourses, Matses people's lives became predicated upon new, water-based forms of sustenance, such as fishing and canoeing, and the river started to replace the forest as the main source of nourishment and means of transportation. Rivers are now central to the everyday life of the Matses, and everyone in the community, including small children, canoes daily to find good fishing spots, to access the cultivated fields and bring back food, to reach forest areas where wild fruit and berries are plentiful, and to find wood and transport it back to the village. Some of the children in the photographs are only toddlers, and yet there are no adults around. Like the *tsësiobo* when they were young, the children are still encouraged to discover the world on their own from as soon as they can walk, and they continue to spend most of their time with their peer group and away from adult supervision, learning to move skillfully and capably through their surroundings. But whereas children *ënden*, in the nomadic past, would play in the forest, today's children are becoming detached from it, growing up as river dwellers rather than forest hunters and trekkers.

In this chapter I want to offer a sense of how children engage with the river and develop affective relationships with it, similarly to how their elders became attached to the forest, and to explore the critical consequences this has on the future of their society at large. To do this, I use photographs taken by the children using digital cameras I distributed during my fieldwork. During my research, the cameras not only created a connection across linguistic barriers, providing a means of sustained engagement with children in a way that interviews did not,

FIGURE 7 *Top row*: children aged three to four play with paddles and canoe on the riverbank (photographs by Elsie, nine years old, and Emanuel, ten). *Bottom row*: boys canoe in the river (photographs by Lily, nine years old, and Nelson, eleven).

but also offered a visual representation of the children's passion for the river. Indeed, almost all the photographs I collected in the field were taken in or around water, while images of the forest were virtually absent. Therefore, these photographs will be used here as the basis for an analysis of the children's predilection for the river and the relevance of this for Matses society as a whole.

Play-Work in the River

When I first arrived in their village, nearly every Matses child asked me the same question: *adac tantanquin tantiec?*, which I soon discovered meant "Can you swim?" The children were suggesting that if I wanted to spend time with them, as I had said to the whole community upon my arrival, I had to be able to move in and around water. Both swimming and canoeing on Amazonian rivers can be arduous and physically demanding: paddles are wrought out of hardwood, heavy and cumbersome, and using them to propel a canoe upstream demands not only skill and technique but also considerable muscular strength. Matses children are extremely dynamic, spending most of each day engaged in physically challenging activities that require agility, skills, and coordination: running around, climbing trees, racing canoes, swimming in the river against the current, jumping from trees into the water, and so forth. This can also be seen as play-work: by having fun with paddles and canoes and by spending much time playing in and around the river, the children become proficient river dwellers who can perform skills that are necessary for survival in their surroundings while also learning the value of *chonuadec*, or hard work.

This kind of practical engagement with the world is embedded within a culturally situated view of childhood and youth that is typical of hunter-gatherer societies and is being passed down between different generations of Matses. Here children are not seen as vulnerable "cherubs"—a term that David Lancy (2008: 2) uses to point out that across Western industrialized contexts, children are seen as being naturally and objectively vulnerable and in constant need of adult supervision. In most hunter-gatherer groups, by contrast, children are encouraged to begin engaging in adult activities and granted a much higher degree of freedom from their earliest years.

As the Matses themselves pointed out to me, this is very different from how *chotac* people, such as myself and those who live in the nearby town and cities, treat children. For a few months during my fieldwork, Soledad, the wife of the village chief and the only *chotac* woman in the community, brought her six-year-old niece Lupe from the city to the village, since her sister (the girl's mother) had to travel elsewhere for work. Having been raised in the city, six-year-old Lupe could not swim, and her aunt forbade her from going alone to the river, where the strong Amazonian currents could have swept her away. Because of this, she was excluded from most of the children's daily play. I would often find Lupe stood on the riverbank on her own, staring gloomily at the crowd of children bathing in deep water in front of her and swimming across from one shore to the other, laughing, splashing, and screaming. I occasionally offered to look after her when she wanted to canoe or be in the water, thereby reproducing a pattern of child-adult interaction that is more typical of industrialized societies where adults are expected to look after children and children's ability to move around depends on their caregivers. But this dynamic is atypical in Matses society, where as soon as they learn to walk children have freedom to access the river and any other spaces they can physically reach.

Hunter-gatherer parents generally do not dedicate much time to explicitly teaching children how to survive in their surroundings, instead "allowing them to (re)discover meanings in the world on their own" (Willerslev 2007: 164). I have often seen two- or three-year-old toddlers in the river unaccompanied, while children from five years old are already skilled at swimming and spend most of their day playing in or near the river together, away from adult supervision. Erik, a two-year-old boy in one of the families I lived with, who could only toddle, could barely talk, and could not swim, would wake up every morning and take himself

FIGURE 8 Children hold machetes, a knife, and a bow and arrow (photographs by Elsie, nine years old, and Diego, twelve).

to the river unaccompanied to wash, play, and socialize with the other children. I would wake up and, not seeing him in the house, ask his mother, "Where is Erik?" and she would look around and scan the house, then nonchalantly ask her other children, "Where is your little brother?" to which they would reply, "He went to the river by himself." To reach the river, Erik had to leave his home, cross part of the village, and then climb down a very steep slope on the riverbank while holding onto small plants along the way, which even I had to walk down carefully for fear of slipping. His parents seemed utterly unconcerned, indeed mildly amused about his journeys to the river.

The children are free not only to roam the world as they please and engage in adult activities but also to use and play with tools that in other societies would be forbidden or actively kept away from them, including knives, guns, machetes, axes, and bows and arrows (as shown in figure 8), as well as other tools that are necessary for subsistence activities such as hooks, lead weights, fishing lines, nets, and so forth.

This high degree of freedom means that while the children must engage in household chores and provide food for themselves (and when they are married, for their families too), they are also free to choose where to go and how to spend their time—and day after day, they choose the river instead of the forest, which represents a profound shift compared with life *ënden*.

Fishing and Becoming *Dadambo*

A consistent proportion of children's time in the water is dedicated to the procurement of protein, which is a daily preoccupation for Amazonian forest dwellers. Both Matses adults and children work hard to this end, reinforcing that "in the family-centered economic system typical of most non-industrialized societies, children are highly valued as current and potential labor" (Gaskins and Paradise 2010: 93). Far from being dependents to be provided for by their parents, as is common across industrialized societies, hunter-gatherer children are generally expected to engage in a physically demanding "chore curriculum" (Lancy 2008: 235) of tasks and activities through which they can help their parents and contribute to the household economy.

For Matses boys this means fishing, weeding and cultivating the fields, chopping firewood, and fetching water from the river, while girls contribute to all of the above, in addition to cooking, tending younger siblings, cleaning plates, and washing clothes. Matses children generally carry out household chores spontaneously and without being asked: when they feel hungry, they go fishing; when water is needed, they collect it from the river; when there is no firewood, they accompany their parents to collect wood from the forest and then chop it up. In general, when their parents ask for help, children rarely refuse or complain, but if they do, the parents will mock them, calling them *bacuëmpi* (little baby) or yell at them for being *chieshe* (lazy), a reprehensible quality in children. Sometimes, as their own parents did to them *ënden*, they will force the children to take *acate* to ensure that they grow strong and willing to work hard.

The set of photographs in figures 9 and 10 show eight-year-old Francisco pulling a large and heavy fishing net out of the water and finding a piranha trapped in it, and then holding a huge catfish that comes up to his chest, which he caught near the village on a different day using fishing hooks. Francisco can stand in perfect balance on the thin gunwale of the canoe, and is even able to walk along it while the canoe is moving, a demonstration of his tremendous physical skills and agility. The boys were feeling hungry, and when children aged seven or eight years old and above feel hungry they do not ask their parents to feed them, but instead go and look for food themselves. Francisco and Diego

FIGURE 9 Francisco, eight years old, checks a net for fish and finds a piranha (photographs by Diego, twelve years old).

FIGURE 10
Francisco holds a
large catfish he has
caught himself
(photograph by
the author).

decided to canoe farther downriver, where Diego's father had previously set up
the net, and after catching the fish they paddled back to the village and handed
it to Diego's mother, who cooked it for them.

Like canoeing, fishing is hard work and requires much strength, agility,
and dynamism. By developing these skills and a hardworking body, Francisco and other Matses boys are becoming *dadambo* (very manly), like Julio,
Leandro, and all the men of previous generations, including Francisco's own
father, Walter, who every day when his son goes to play or fish in the river treks
in the forest and looks for game animals and plants that he can use to heal various illnesses.

Here a particular kind of Matses masculinity is being enacted but also trans-
formed; for whereas Francisco gets up in the morning and heads out to the
river, his father, Walter, will trek deep into the forest and Francisco will rarely,

if ever, follow him. For Francisco's generation, being *dadambo* no longer encompasses the physical know-how of the forest, good marksmanship, and the mastery of hunting skills and instead pertains solely to the skills and prowess of the river, which can be understood both as the response to environmental constraints and as an active choice by the younger generation.

Similar to boys, who should become *dadambo* from a young age, girls are actively encouraged to develop skills and engage in forms of labor that will make them *dayac*, a term that can be translated as "hardworking" and refers to a female-specific quality denoting physical strength, industriousness, and a tireless will to perform the tough work required by the household economy that runs through all generations of Matses women. Here there is also a kind of continuity with the past insofar as by helping their mothers with a range of household activities such as cooking, washing up, cleaning, and looking after younger siblings, girls as young as four years old actively perpetuate a *dayac* attitude that is seen as constitutive of womanhood.

Portrayed as quintessentially female, these tasks have been traditionally opposed to men's primary role as providers of protein, which in the Matses hunting economy created a kind of reciprocity whereby women would primarily contribute through harvesting the fields and cooking food, while men provided meat. During his fieldwork in the 1970s, Steven Romanoff (1983) observed that Matses women had an active role in hunting but that this only involved accompanying the men, helping them to spot animals and carrying home the prey. A woman would by no means trek on her own and catch animals by herself, meaning that men were effectively the sole protein providers, and women's roles were complementary to this.

But as fishing began to replace hunting as the primary source of protein income, the role of women also began to shift. Through fishing, girls from the age of eight or even younger are able to provide protein for themselves, in the same way as the boys and often with even better results. Also, unlike the boys, girls are taught from a very young age to prepare and cook food, which is seen as a female task, meaning that they can complete the whole end-to-end cycle of protein procurement and preparation on their own, without having to rely on men at any stage. The set of photographs in figure 11 show Matses girls completing the whole fishing cycle—Maryam is digging for baitworms with a machete; Romina looks bored while she waits for a fish to bite the baitworm; and having caught a fish, Inés is gutting it with her bare hands without even using a knife. Afterward the girls, who are as young as seven, will go home and cook the fish themselves. Accordingly, if "children's ongoing presence and integration in adult activities is related to the society's mode of economic production" (Gaskins 2003: 250), in Matses society the role of children is changing along with the transformation of their economy and the ongoing transition from hunting to fishing.

FIGURE 11 Girls fishing (photographs by Matilda, ten years old, and Elsie, nine).

Almost Hunters

The images in figure 12 are among the very few I collected that show children hunting rather than fishing. Two boys, Nelson and Pablo, are in bushy areas a very short distance behind their houses, holding a *uasha* (*puma garza* in Spanish), a large bird they caught with bows and arrows while playing, as their parents and grandparents did when they themselves were children. The boys showed me the photographs with great pride: it is unusual for them to catch a bird of this size, and while Matses boys still play with bows and arrows, during many years of fieldwork I have never seen them catch anything beyond much smaller birds.

Unlike the children *ënden*, the boys rarely if ever venture into the forest to hunt bigger animals, and their play with bows and arrows never develops into play-work allowing them to foster productive hunting or tracking skills, as was the case for their grandfathers. On my sporadic walks through the forest with children, teenagers, or even young people in their twenties, it was visible even to me how limited their forest skills and knowledge are compared with those of their elders. While the *tsësiobo* woke me up before dawn, when the air is still cold, my treks with younger people only took place later in the morning and were much shorter in time and distance—mainly because young people, even those

FIGURE 12 Boys catch a bird (photographs by Nelson, eleven years old, and Paco, ten).

in their late teens or early twenties, are generally scared of the forest and quickly get bored of trekking. The elders can trek for hours without feeling tired or becoming disoriented, whereas children and teenagers get bored quickly, turning back as soon as the trees become thicker for fear of getting lost. Halfway through my fieldwork, two eighteen-year-old boys left on a hunt and didn't come back at night, causing much preoccupation among their families. Leandro, their elderly uncle who was born before contact—the elderly man who used to get his arms covered in poisonous ants—went out to look for them, fearing they might be lost. He trekked for hours in the dark, demonstrating his much better orienteering and tracking skills, and found the boys camping in a hunting hut that Leandro and other elders have set up deeper in the rainforest. The boys had lost their way and somehow ended up there, they said, and were then too scared to walk back in the dark. They had not even managed to catch any meat, which would never have happened to the elders if they had trekked that far.

On one occasion I went trekking with Riqui, Julio's sixteen-year-old son, who gathered up a group of younger boys and offered to show me the forest as his father had done. As we walked, Riqui entertained the group by mimicking his father, pointing at random trees and plants we walked by, shouting out their names and medicinal uses, as his father always does when he walks in the forest with the children. Riqui's impression also mocked the elderly people's harsh, thick way of talking, which I often struggled to understand. Soon the forest around us was echoing with the children's laughter, and the boys turned to me and shouted, "*moiqui nec*, Camilla!" meaning "He's just kidding": Riqui had no idea of what all the different trees and plants are called, and he was just making them up. When I asked him what the real name of this or that tree was, he shrugged and shouted in a funny voice, "*tsaun!*" (I have no idea), and the others shouted out in response, "*tantiadenquio icquec!*" (He doesn't have a clue). The trek was exceptionally short and ended with the children's stock response whenever they get bored or want to play: "*cho nesnu*" (Let's go wash in the river).

When I asked why they seldom walk through the forest with older people, Matses girls and boys alike replied" "*chieshebi*," which can be translated as "I'm lazy" or, better, "It's too much effort," and "*dacuëdenquiembi*," "I'm scared" of the forest, as in the dialogue below with sixteen-year-old Riqui.

CAMILLA: Have you ever been hunting?

RIQUI: Yes, I went once.

CAMILLA: Only once?

RIQUI: Twice [he giggles].

CAMILLA: What did you catch?

RIQUI: Nothing. There weren't any [i.e., game animals].

CAMILLA: Why don't you go more often?

RIQUI: It's full of snakes, the forest. I'm scared. It's too much effort.

At Riqui's age, his father, Julio, was living nomadically in the deep rainforest and was not only a skilled forest dweller and hunter but also an experienced warrior taking part in raids. By contrast, Riqui and children of his generation are showing a disengagement with the forest that is to a large extent an active choice: as I have shown, the children are free to explore the world as they please, and every morning when Julio and the other elders go hunting or trekking, their children and grandchildren could follow them and learn about the forest, but they prefer not to because, in their own words, "it's too much effort."

Yet this choice can only be understood as an act of negotiation with the challenges posed by sedentary life on the river. After settling along riverbanks, Matses society experienced a dramatic demographic expansion, and the rapid growth of villages led to the depletion of game animals nearby. The village where

I worked was founded in the early 1990s, and people say that at that time there were plenty of game animals, meaning that they could trek a short distance and come back with plenty of meat. But the Matses kept hunting every day, as they had always done when living nomadically in the rainforest, and prey animals moved farther away, so that now even the most skilled older hunters could trek for miles and still come home empty-handed.

Moreover, soon after missionary contact, the Matses stopped hunting with bows and arrows and started using shotguns instead, which are louder and over time push animals away. They are also costly; cartridges were initially provided and brought in regularly by the missionaries, but when the missionaries left Matses territory in the early 2000s, cartridges became much harder to procure. While shotguns are durable and every family owns at least one, cartridges have to be purchased in the city with money and as such are always in short supply. Becoming a good hunter is complicated not only by the scarcity of game animals but also by the shortage of cartridges, thus adding an economic to an ecological obstacle.

In response, Matses people began to use fishing as an easier source of protein, and now all generations are extremely skilled at it. But whereas the elders prefer to hunt and only use fishing as a last resort if they cannot find meat, hungry children go straight to the river. The children say that hunting is boring because there are no animals around, whereas fishing is much easier (to everyone's great surprise, even I was able to get the hang of it after a while) and generally more fruitful—it is rare to return empty-handed from the river. Several of the boys told me they would like to try hunting with shotguns, but cartridges are a precious resource and if a family gets hold of any, they will be used by the elderly men, who are better hunters. This leads to something of a catch-22 situation, where boys are not given cartridges because they are not good hunters, but with no cartridges with which to practice, they never become good at hunting and, more importantly, never develop the same kind of affective engagement with the forest as their elders.

Children's inability to hunt is to an extent an adaptive response—the children have to adjust to a landscape that has been altered and compromised by the actions of past generations, who after settling down in permanent villages kept hunting relentlessly as they did when they were nomadic but without a conservation strategy or plan. Tim Ingold proposes that landscapes are always transforming as a result of human activities that take place within them and can therefore be seen as material evidence of the past. In his words, a landscape is "an enduring record of, and a testimony to, the lives and works of past generations who have dwelt within it, and in so doing, have left there something of themselves" (1993: 152). His view is echoed in the anthropology of Amazonia by Laura Rival, who argues that for the Huaorani people of Ecuador, "trekking in the forest is like walking in a living history book in which natural history and human history merge seamlessly" (2002: 2). But whereas Ingold's view of the landscape likens the social life of the people who dwell within it to an "orchestral performance" in which "the gestures of the performers may be said to resonate with each other" (1993: 160), the impact of the short-term sustenance strategies of past generations on Matses people's current environments has generated more of a dissonance—one to which the children must now adjust.

A Passion for Water

Matses children have a clear passion for the river, spending most of their time in it and turning the riverine landscape into a playground. Nearby trees become springboards for them to climb up and jump down into the water. When the river level lowers in the dry season and sandy beaches appear along the banks, the children spend hours playing on them, using wet sand to build houses or to bury themselves (and me, whenever I am there) with it. The canoes that adults use solely for transport are used for racing or for make-believe journeys to the world of the *chotac*. The children call to each other, scream, and laugh loudly, and all day long, from every part of the village, adults can hear the echo of the children's laughter as they play in the river. The photographs in figure 13 show the river as a playground in the children's own perspectives and from a multiplicity of angles: from the banks, looking at one's peers in the water; from ground level looking up to others climbing a tree to jump in; from up a tree looking at other children jumping down; from the water's surface looking toward the bank; and even from underwater.

FIGURE 13 Girls and boys play in the river (photographs by Edgar, ten years old; Nelson, eleven; Rebeca, ten; and Diego, twelve).

FIGURE 14 Raúl crafts a canoe in the forest (photograph by Flora, twelve years old).

Elderly men and women are skilled at riverine activities but have never developed the same passion for the river environment as the younger generations who have grown up around it. This is especially the case for the older men, since they generally spend even more time in the forest than the women, as exemplified by Raúl, who, in the photograph in figure 14, taken by his twelve-year-old daughter Flora, is captured crafting a canoe for his family of two wives and eleven children.

Raúl was born and grew up deep in the rainforest, when Matses people kept away from navigable watercourses for fear of the *chotac* who dwelled along them. Unlike Flora and his other children, who grew up in a world where the river was already central to life, Raúl had never even seen a river until his teens, when his own father took him on a two-day trek to the banks of a wide Amazonian tributary to see the *acte dapa* (the "big water," an expression that Matses people sometimes use to refer to the Yaquerana River, which is much wider than the creek the village is built along and leads toward *chotac* territory).

He still recounts the feelings of fear, astonishment, and trepidation at seeing such a wide body of water for the first time, and when a dolphin broke the surface and spouted water into the air, he thought, "This must be a deadly spirit!"

Later in life, when he was already an adult, Raúl and his generation started to settle along riverbanks and became familiar with the river environment. Raúl became very skilled at fishing and canoeing and knowledgeable about riverine life and fauna, and even learned how to craft canoes using hardwood and machetes, as shown in the photograph taken by his daughter. But having developed these skills later in life, Raúl and his generation never became as fond of the river as they are of the forest—especially the elderly men. They say that fishing is *chieshe* (boring) because "you sit on a canoe all day without moving," and they do not even see fish as proper food compared with meat. To them, the river is an easy source of protein and a necessary means of transport, but they keep walking through the forest every day to gather wild food and hunt, and only if they come home empty handed from the hunt will they go fishing in the river at dusk.

I often joined Raúl's and other families on daylong fishing trips, where we would leave the village before sunrise and canoe far upriver, where the riverbed is wider and the fish are more abundant, before arriving back at the village at dusk, exhausted but cheerful, with a canoe full of the day's catch. Children take an active part in these trips: they help set up the canoe, dig for baitworms, fish with hooks and line, gut the fish, collect wood, make a fire, and help to cook lunch. Elderly men join the trip and drive the canoe, but they often bring their guns and, while the women and children fish on the river, go hunting in the nearby forest.

On one of these trips, Raúl decided to sit with us on the canoe and fish for a while. We all sat quietly on the canoe that was floating on the still river, tied with a piece of rope to a tree on the riverbank, everyone holding a fishing line with a hook attached to it. We each grabbed one of the baitworms that the children had dug out in the village and put into a plastic container, stuck the worm onto the hook, and threw the line into the water, waiting for the fish to bite—a slow process that requires much time waiting in silence and sitting still in a small space. Raúl became impatient very quickly. He would throw his hook into the water, and after a few seconds, allowing barely any time for the fish to bite the hook, he would pull it back up and look at the intact bait, sighing with frustration and moving impatiently, very much like a bored child in school. "This is boring," he kept saying, and "I'm not catching anything!," acting childishly and playfully to try to catch the attention of his wife, who kept ignoring him because she was too concentrated on fishing. Eventually he took his shotgun and went hunting in the nearby forest by himself. He came back several hours later carrying two dead monkeys.

Both Matses children and elders know the names and habits of fish or have practical know-how regarding canoeing and fishing, but knowing is inseparable from the emotional moods and modalities through which it unfolds (Harris 2007), so while all generations are skilled at riverine activities and even dependent on them, the key difference lies not so much in *what* the children and the elders know but in *how* they know it. As they express it themselves, the children are learning to know the forest through boredom, fear, and laziness, whereas for the elders the forest is thrilling, exciting, and rewarding. On the other hand, children's daily engagement with the river unfolds through play, laughter, and fun from their earliest years of life—and by learning to know and engage with the landscape differently to older generations, the children are actively driving a process of social and environmental transformation.

The Forest Behind, the River Ahead

The intergenerational differences in attitudes to the environment became clearer than ever when I joined a group of four families on a weeklong trip to Añushiyacu, a small hunting settlement deep in the forest, a day's walk from the village, where game animals are still abundant. The settlement consists of one big longhouse, the traditional *maloca*, surrounded by a small cultivation of manioc and plantains, built in a small, cleared area in the middle of the rainforest close to a small creek. In response to protein scarcity, Matses elders trek to Añushiyacu at least once every two months, and they come back a few days later bringing plenty of meat. Children and young people occasionally accompany them, but are rarely keen—when I went, however, a few teenage girls and a group of children joined the trip, as they often would when I was involved. During the day, the children and I stayed at home with the women, while the men, most of whom were born before missionary contact, left the longhouse at dawn and came back in the afternoon with leaf baskets full of animals: monkeys, deer, sloths, armadillos, and more. When we heard the men coming back, we all rushed to see what they had brought, and the women screamed with excitement and ran toward the hunters to take the catch off their hands and start skinning it for cooking.

I had never seen hunters coming back with so much meat to the village, where they often returned from long treks with empty hands and a look of disappointment, saying to their family waiting back home, "*nidbëdec*" (There wasn't any). But in Añushiyacu a fire burned throughout the day in the longhouse and we all sat around it, eating meat and waiting for the hunters to bring more. The elders came back pumped up with adrenaline and, after having trekked all day, went out again in the evening to poison the creek with the *ancueste* root, staying there until late at night before bringing back baskets full of fish. Afterward, we slept on hammocks in the longhouse set at close distance from one another, and if someone snored too loudly the person next to them would wake up and perhaps make a joke, waking up someone else who did the same until the whole house was awake, making jokes and laughing, and eventually we all fell back asleep and everything was silent once more. "This is how we lived *ënden*," the elders said to me, and the atmosphere was so cheerful, and food so abundant, that even I felt nostalgic at the thought of a past I had never known.

The children and teenagers who had joined the trip, including fifteen-year-old Nancy and sixteen-year-old Tina, felt very differently. Nancy spent nearly her whole week in Añushiyacu lying on a hammock, barely helping her mother,

Serena, and certainly not sharing her enthusiasm. Normally, Serena would have told her off and asked her to help, but she was so excited about all the food being caught by her husband that she barely paid attention to her daughter. Nancy was also happy to eat meat, but she kept repeating all day long that she was *chieshpambo* (painfully bored), begging her mother to let her go back to the village and blaming me for this unbearable boredom. "Camilla, if it wasn't for you, I wouldn't be here. I'd be in the village, playing volleyball. I'm only here because you came. [Putting on a high-pitch, child-like moaning voice:] Mum, come on, let's go back. Let's go back, mum! [Her mother ignores her, and she goes back to her normal voice.] Camilla, ask my mum to go back. They will take you, if you ask! I want to play volleyball. I am *so* bored!"

Diego, who is twelve years old, also joined the trip and went hunting with the men for the first couple of days, but then got bored and stayed at home with us. He kept asking me why I hadn't brought my laptop.

DIEGO: Why haven't you brought your laptop? I want to watch a film!

CAMILLA: There's no solar panel here! Why don't you go hunting with your father?

DIEGO: Nah, I can't be bothered today!

CAMILLA: Why not?

DIEGO: They'll walk very far! It's tiring. It's too much effort.

The younger generations are developing a taste for certain leisure activities that Matses people learned from the *chotac*, such as playing volleyball and football, or watching television. Every day, at dusk, young women gather at the center of the village to play volleyball and young men to play football, surrounded by an audience of villagers. Only people from about seventeen years of age up to thirty-five take part in the games, while older people show no interest in them. The younger children watch, occasionally engaging in side-games of football and volleyball with old, broken balls, all longing for the day when they will reach puberty and be finally allowed to play with the adults. The elders are extremely critical, describing volleyball and football as useless activities performed *ambembi*, "just for the sake of it" or "for fun" without any tangible outcome or purpose. As such they stand in contrast to hunting, trekking or collecting medicinal plants, which are productive and contribute to the economy of sustenance. But for the younger generations, it seems, living without volleyball and football is painfully boring.

The same goes for watching movies, which elderly people also consider a way of being lazy and unproductive. Since there is no electricity in the village, the children can rarely watch television, mostly on their occasional visits to Colonia Angamos. A few young men have also bought small projectors and DVD players in the city to watch films in their houses back in the village, but these break easily and are powered by gasoline, which is always in short supply. The children often asked me to show a movie on my laptop, and I often accommodated their requests, as shown in the following excerpt from my fieldnotes.

> I'm lying on a hammock, worn out by the afternoon heat, going through my notes. The children come looking for me, as usual. Diego leads the crowd and insists that I show a movie on my laptop. "Let's watch a film!" he says. I stand up from the hammock and turn on my laptop, to the cheers of Diego and other children, and we sit in the shade behind the house. A crowd of children sit as close as possible to the very small screen, looking extremely concentrated and still and quiet, which they very rarely are. All of a sudden, all the children, together and at the very same time, jump up and take flight, running. Some of them scream, *choec, choec!* "He is coming!" I turn around and see Raúl, Diego's father, approaching us, with his silent hunter moves. I wouldn't have noticed him was it not for the children's breakaway—they may not be hunters but they are still exceptionally skilled at catching every detail around them. Raúl holds a burning stick in one hand and another stick with frog poison in the other. He is threatening the children with the poison. If he manages to grab one, he will burn the child's arm and put poison on it—even on his own son, Diego. But by the time he gets to us, the children have vanished.

Raúl and the other elders were unhappy with the children watching movies in full daylight rather than working, which can turn them lazy. When threatening them with poison, which is seen as transmitting energy and the will to work hard, Raúl would remind the children of the value of physical labor and condemn their laziness. Although the elders never complained to me directly, after a few of these raids I decided only to show movies at night, when children are not required to carry out housework activities. This caused many complaints from the children—especially Diego, who made it clear that he would have much rather been watching movies than hunting with his father at Añushiyacu.

The expeditions to Añushiyacu are an expression of a fairly common adaptive response to meat scarcity employed by hunter-gatherers after sedentarization, whereby hunting settlements are established in locations where meat is still abundant and a smaller group of skilled hunters in the community travels there occasionally and then shares the meat with the rest of the community. Nevertheless, for Matses elders this is clearly not a purely functional activity but also one that arises from and sustains their affective relationship with the forest. In Añushiyacu the forest remains a giving environment, and mobility is not a response to necessity but rather a sensorially and emotionally rewarding activity through which they engage meaningfully with their surroundings.

When I asked the elders why they don't move back to Añushiyacu, they replied that it is too far from the nearest town, where they occasionally need to buy manufactured goods such as cartridges, as well as from the nearest hospital. The current positions of the villages represent an acceptable compromise for the elders, sitting halfway between the deep forest and the land of the *chotac*, allowing them to reach both when needed. But the young are becoming increasingly dissatisfied with the village, and living near the inland forest no longer seems to be a requirement for either girls or boys, as Nancy and Diego made explicit during our trip there.

Both Nancy and Diego told me that in the future they want to move even farther away from the current position of the village, toward wider rivers where fish are plentiful and the land of the *chotac* within ever-closer reach. While fish remain available and more abundant than meat, they are nonetheless diminishing in the waters near the village. This is because Matses people have been poisoning the river with the *ancueste* root, having no long-term conservation plan, just as was the case with hunting. Nancy said, "When I'm older I'll move closer to the Yaquerana River," the wide body of water closer to the town of Colonia Angamos and the gateway to *chotac* territory.

Children's passion for the river is driving them farther down the *acte dapa*. This has clear implications for the whole of Matses society: by growing up as river dwellers instead of forest trekkers, Matses children are closing off the possibility of a future economy based on hunting, foraging, and trekking, and are leaving forest knowledge behind. At the same time, the river-futures they are moving toward are entwined with new economic practices and inseparable from certain kinds of *chotac* lifestyles, objects, and practices that children yearn for—including money and monetary exchange, which is the focus of the next chapter.

3

The Sound of Inequality

Children as Agents of Economic Change

Edgar (ten) is taking photographs while four other boys—Diego (twelve), Francisco (ten), Nelson (eleven), and Emanuel (ten)—stand outside the house of Enrique, the village chief and schoolteacher, and three of them stare through his window (figure 15). Inside the house, Enrique is distributing money to people who have done work for him and receiving payments from those who have debts. He sits on a chair at his desk, using a calculator to count the money owed and manage the payments, writing his sums in a notebook to keep the count, while speaking his calculations out loud. On his desk, next to the notebook, is a little pile of notes and coins: a rare sight in Matses communities. At the entrance of the room stands a queue of people, both men and women, who wait to hand over or receive their money. They approach Enrique one by one and stand next to his chair as he hands out the cash. They all move slowly and speak quietly, creating a strange contrast with Enrique's confident manner and loud tone. Much like the sight of money, the silence enfolding the whole scene is unique in an Amazonian village, where from the earliest hours of the day the air resonates with the sound of axes chopping firewood, people calling each other, babies crying, elders chanting, and above all the sound of children's play and laughter that echoes all day long around the houses. Children are not allowed in Enrique's room, except for babies or toddlers who come in with their mothers, and they must be silent; if they say a word, laugh, or scream loudly, as they usually do, the adults will yell at them and force them to leave. The boys thus stand outside, quietly, looking in through the window.

The ongoing changes in Matses society cannot be understood without considering the recent yet striking impact of money, trade, and the market economy on their everyday lives. Money started circulating in Matses communities only in

50

FIGURE 15 Boys look at money through a window (photograph by Edgar, ten years old).

the past twenty years or so but has quickly become of paramount concern to adults and children alike. While their subsistence is still based on hunting, fishing, horticulture, and the use of natural resources available in their surroundings, Matses people are now dependent on an array of manufactured goods that can only be purchased using cash, such as cartridges, fishing tools, gasoline, machetes, metal pots, clothes, and pharmaceuticals. And yet cash is always in short supply, or as they say on a daily basis, "*piucquid nidbëdec*" (There's no money), and the little that is available is unequally distributed, leading to unprecedented inequalities based on monetary wealth and challenging established moral values and practices, including children's role in the household economy.

The image of Matses boys denied access to the money-room, reduced to staring at cash transactions through the window, is in marked contrast to those shown in the previous chapter of them handling knives or fishing unsupervised in the river—suggesting that the introduction of cash has created adult-exclusive spaces and promoted the diffusion of new economic practices which, unlike providing food or helping with chores, Matses children are not encouraged to master. Indeed, a number of ethnographers have documented that when societies transition from a hunter-gatherer economy to one based on trade and monetary transactions, children begin to be excluded from economic activity (see Lancy 1996; Rival 2002). The introduction of money is often entwined with that of formal schooling, meaning that children shift from being active food providers who hunt and fish for food to becoming pupils to be provided for by their moneymaking parents.

In Matses society, children's exclusion from the money economy is twofold: children have little if any access to cash because money is almost absent but also because the little available is handled almost exclusively by the adults. And yet, I argue that from their peripheral position, Matses children are nevertheless driving ongoing processes of economic change, playing a dynamic and crucial role in the transition from a hunter-gatherer economy of subsistence toward one based on trade and monetary exchange. This means recognizing that children are "active economic agents" (Zelizer 2002: 377) who can have direct impact onto the economy even when they seem to have little or no direct access to it. Matses children have no direct access to money, which is often not even available to their parents, let alone the children themselves. But simply by placing value on money and turning it into an object of desire and a key target for their future, while shifting away from the traditional economic choices of their elders and the moral values associated with it, the children are transforming their social economy and its possible future developments.[1]

The Introduction of Money into Matses Society: A Brief History

Money was first brought into Matses communities by the missionaries, who also initiated the Matses to the basics of monetary exchange. The missionaries would buy handicraft products such as bows and arrows, and with the money earned from the transaction, the Matses could in turn buy manufactured goods and medicines from them. Within a short period of time they became reliant on manufactured goods, but money only started circulating more widely and consistently in the 1990s. Even people in their thirties and forties recount that in their youth, money was not very relevant and was even less available than it is today.

The missionaries also taught Matses people reading, writing, and mathematics until the 1980s, when the Peruvian government set up state-run schools in every Matses community and offered training to a few Matses adults to study in Iquitos and become schoolteachers. The introduction of schooling led to increased circulation of Peruvian currency in Matses communities, as well as unprecedented forms of social differentiation based on the unequal distribution of monetary wealth, since Matses teachers receive a fixed salary from the Ministry of Education of approximately 3,000–3,500 Peruvian nuevo soles per month (about 790–920 US dollars), which is an inordinate amount of money for a Matses person. Representing a tiny proportion of society, with an average of two teachers for a village of two hundred people, schoolteachers have become an elite due to their wealth and the privileged lifestyle it enables (see Gasché 1997; Trapnell 2008). Their government salaries allow them to travel to the city regularly and enjoy its luxuries, such as dining out and shopping, whereas most Matses people earn only small and irregular amounts of cash by selling handicrafts during their expensive, infrequent visits to distant *chotac* settlements and often cannot even afford to buy clothes for their children or modest outboard motors for their canoes.

In the village where I have conducted most of my research, this new kind of wealth divide is demonstrated by the status of the village chief, Enrique, who was my first host during my fieldwork and remains one of my closest Matses friends. Enrique was born in 1969, the year of missionary contact, and as such belongs to the first generation of Matses who never experienced nomadic life in the forest, growing up in in a sedentary village where contact with *chotac* people was already established. He received formal education from childhood and not only enjoyed reading and writing but even preferred it to traditional activities— unlike most of his peers and his older siblings, who grew up in the rainforest and found formal education tedious and not as relevant or satisfying as walking through the forest, cultivating a field, collecting wild fruit, and hunting.

When he grew up, Enrique was among the very few Matses men who in their early twenties traveled to Iquitos to study and become schoolteachers. His father, Isaías, was critical of this decision; being a fierce warrior and an experienced hunter, who grew up before missionary contact when Matses people "lived without clothes," as he says himself, Isaías regarded education as a waste of time. "My father didn't understand the importance of schooling," says Enrique. "He took me and my siblings to walk through the forest and work in the field. My siblings liked it, but I didn't. I preferred studying in school." His father told him off and called him *chieshe* (lazy), but Enrique kept studying and was later hired by the Ministry of Education to teach in his home village in the forest. When he started earning money from teaching, his father changed his mind. "Now I buy things for my father. Axes, knives, clothes, soap. He's happy that I'm a teacher now. Now he thinks that schooling is good," says Enrique. His siblings skipped classes but always helped with the housework, like most of today's children still do. "Now they have no money!" says Enrique, grinning with pride. "What good has cultivating the field done them?"

Like most schoolteachers of his generation, Enrique cannot hunt and fish as proficiently as his peers, who have spent more time in the forest, and he doesn't do so very often, as he spends most of his time teaching classes or traveling to town. However, schoolteachers are competent at a whole range of *chotac* activities that most Matses people struggle with, such as speaking Spanish, relating to the *chotac*, using technologies such as phones and the internet in town, and of course making and managing money. Some schoolteachers, like Enrique, started setting up small stores in their houses, where they sell clothes, fishing hooks and line, flip-flops, flashlights, sweets, school materials, and other manufactured goods. They buy these in the city with the money earned through teaching and sell them in the village at a much higher price to make a profit—a type of business they learned by watching shopkeepers in town and which Matses people perceive as quintessentially *chotac*: the notion of making a profit, saving, storing up goods, and accumulating wealth stand in marked opposition to the give-and-take values of the hunting economy, where the ability to share one's catch is a source of pride and prestige. For the older generations, as described previously, skilled hunters were desirable husbands and had several wives precisely due to their ability to catch plenty of meat and share it with their large families.

In addition to his shop, Enrique has set up a business through which he sells the black juice that Matses people used to tattoo their bodies—produced from the fruits of *chëshëte*, the "genipap tree"—to artists in Los Angeles, who buy it to make temporary tattoos. When the artists place an order, Enrique commissions a crew of Matses men and women in the village to collect *chëshëte* fruits and process the juice, and when the juice is ready he takes it to Iquitos and dispatches it to the United States. The tattoo artists send money back to Enrique, who collects it in Iquitos and returns to the village to pay off the people who have worked for him. People who help out receive a fee from Enrique, who pays the workers from his house in the village. However, since most of the villagers have tabs open at his shop, Enrique will count how much money he owes the workers and how much they owe him for previous purchases, and he will then close the tab and pay them any difference. People are often left disappointed and complain that his business is unfair, but they continue to take part, since this is one of the very few means of earning some cash. Enrique, on the other hand, complains that people always ask him to give them goods *ambembi* (for free), and nobody understands that running a business is hard work and money does not simply materialize in his pockets.

Enrique's success in the *chotac* world extends to the woman he married, Consuelo, who was born and grew up in the city, Iquitos. The two met in the city when Enrique was studying to become a teacher. For a Matses man, marrying a *chotac* woman and taking her back to his village is something to be proud of and inspires a great deal of admiration from others. But marrying a *chotac* woman is not straightforward and requires particular skills and resources. As people in the village say, Enrique was able to woo Consuelo only because he spoke Spanish fluently and knew how to deal with the *chotac* and how to approach women by making conversation and flirting.

In the photograph shown in figure 15, the boys are watching Enrique managing his business and paying off the people who have processed the juice for him, using a calculator to subtract what they owe him. In the very same room where money appears in front of the children's fascinated eyes, a plethora of goods—clothes, knives, matches, candles, shoes, pots, flashlights, and more—stand heaped on shelves, piled on the floor, or hung from nails on the walls, mimicking the aesthetic of the shops run by *chotac* people in the town, Colonia Angamos. The children's exclusion from adult spaces is unusual in Matses society, where, as I have discussed, they are generally allowed access to any social space and activity. It is from this marginal position that Matses children are learning not just to see cash as an object of desire, but also to perceive that *piucquid nidbëdec*, and Matses people are poor.

Children's Awareness of Economic Exclusion

The emerging and fast-growing forms of wealth-divide and economic inequality in Matses communities are graphically rendered in the drawings of ten-year-old Edgar showing Matses people traveling on their motorized canoes to Colonia Angamos (figure 16). The first image shows simple Matses, who have no specific names and only average-sized motors. The second represents Tito, a Matses leader and schoolteacher who, through his frequent travels and exchanges with *chotac* people, managed to obtain a political position in the regional administration of Colonia Angamos, whose jurisdiction includes Matses communities—meaning that Matses people are required to vote in the elections for the local mayor held every four years. Given that as a bloc Matses people represent the majority of the electorate, *chotac* candidates always look to include Matses representatives on their slates to gain more votes.

Earning both a teacher's salary and one for his political role, Tito has become wealthy and famous among the Matses. As shown in the drawing, he owns a large canoe with a Jonson motor, an expensive and noisy type of engine, and when he travels back to Matses territory from his frequent journeys to the *chotac* world, he is preceded by the loud noise of his motorized canoe, which can be heard from far away and is immediately recognizable. When they hear its roar, children in the village run toward the river, screaming, "*Tito chue, Tito chue*" (Tito is coming), and stand on the banks to watch his impressive canoe pass by, fast and packed with plastic bags full of the goods he brings from the city.

Much like the silence in Enrique's house when he hands out money, the roar of Tito's Jonson motor becomes a tangible sound of inequality, a reminder of the uneven distribution of wealth among Matses people, as the children themselves put into words. When discussing his drawing, Edgar explained: "Tito has a lot of money! He has a Jonson motor and he goes to town all the time to buy clothes and rice. My dad doesn't have a Jonson motor. He doesn't have any money."

Edgar's father, Clemente, is a man in his mid-forties, born at the time of missionary contact, and therefore belongs to the same generation as Enrique, the village chief and schoolteacher, and Tito. But unlike them, Clemente never enjoyed schooling and became a skilled hunter instead—like his own father, who was born many years before contact and was a skilled forest-dweller and fierce warrior. I once saw Clemente come back from a hunt carrying five large

FIGURE 16 *Above*: Anonymous Matses people travel on their modest motorized canoes. *Below*: Tito, a wealthy Matses chief, on his Jonson-motorized canoe (drawing by Edgar, ten years old).

peccaries on his canoe, looking proud and exhausted, and cheered by his children and his wife, who quickly proceeded to cut the meat and share it with other villagers.

But Clemente and his family also feel the need for money, and like other men of his age, in the past Clemente has spent time in Colonia Angamos working as a builder, where he was befriended by a local politician and, like Tito, was invited to take part as a councilor in the regional municipality. However, unlike Tito and other schoolteachers, Clemente does not speak Spanish very well and is not as experienced and familiar with the *chotac* lifestyles and working environments. Given the high levels of corruption in local municipalities, Matses people involved in political activities often end up with financial and legal problems, and Clemente is an example of this: the politician who had offered him work tried to misappropriate part of his salary, and when Clemente sued him he made a counter-allegation against Clemente, accusing him of stealing money. Clemente returned to his village with no savings, no goods bought in the city, no job, and a legal charge of theft. He now lives in the village with his family and rarely travels to *chotac* towns.

Edgar is therefore growing up in a family where money is seen as necessary but is scarce or unavailable in its material form of paper and coins, and the household is almost entirely founded on a subsistence economy of hunting, fishing, and horticulture. Money is a nevertheless tangible presence in Edgar's imagination, and he frequently refers to it when playing, drawing, and interacting with other children. One day I saw Edgar in a group of girls and boys playing a game that consisted of chasing each other and trying to steal pieces of crumpled-up paper from one another. As they ran around, grabbing each other's arms and filling the air all around with laughter, the children were screaming, "*Chinerita*, give me your *chinerita!*" When I asked them what *chinerita* meant, they showed me their pieces of paper and said, "This is *chinerita*! It's *chinero*," which I eventually understood to be how they were pronouncing the Spanish word *dinero*, "money," providing an example of how, through playing, children appropriate objects and practices that pertain to the domain of adults and are precluded to them.

Money often appears in Matses children's daily games, dialogues, and drawings, as shown by ten-year-old Emanuel (figure 17). In his drawing, Emanuel imagines himself buying *curichi*, a kind of popsicle that is very popular with children, in a shop in Colonia Angamos. Unlike the shop run by Enrique in the village, the shops in town are always full of people coming in to buy goods and display many more items, including *chotac* food the children love: freshly baked bread, sweets, lollipops, rice, biscuits, and fizzy drinks have a unique taste compared with Matses dietary staples, which lack any sweet and sugary flavor, and the children often associate being in Colonia Angamos with the possibility of eating this *chotac* food, as suggested by the following dialogue between myself, Emanuel, and his nine-year-old sister, Elsie.

ELSIE: They sell so many things there! [i.e., in Colonia Angamos].

CAMILLA: What do they sell?

ELSIE: Clothes, flashlights, shoes, bread.

EMANUEL: Sunglasses!

ELSIE: Sunglasses! Buy us some, Camilla!

CAMILLA: All right. Did you buy anything in Colonia Angamos?

EMANUEL: No! I have no money.

CAMILLA: And your parents? Did they buy you anything?

EMANUEL: They have no money either.

FIGURE 17 Emanuel buys food in town (drawing by Emanuel, ten years old).

ELSIE: Emanuel wanted to steal bread, but he was scared of the police! [They both laugh.]

CAMILLA: Why did you want to steal?!

EMANUEL: Because I have no money!

ELSIE: Matses people have no money, Camilla.

By imagining money, and placing value on it as they do so, the children are turning it into a concrete target for their future adulthoods—as can be seen by the activities of the older children, who are rejecting much of the knowledge of older generations but are already seeking ways to become money makers.

The (Im)possibilities of Making Money

At some point during my fieldwork, a new store popped up in the village. It was opened by two boys: Diego, twelve, the boy who joined the hunting trip to Añush-iyacu, and his older brother Mateo, sixteen. They opened it in the house of Mateo, who as a teenage unmarried man lives on his own but still contributes to his parents' household economy. The store was a replica of the one set up by Enrique in his own house, but unlike the abundance of goods Enrique can afford through his teacher's salary and profitable business, the boys' shop had only a few items on display: two T-shirts, one skirt, a few bars of soap, and some cheap flashlights. Their goods ran out quickly, and after only a few days the boys were out of business.

At their age, both Diego and Mateo take a daily and consistent part in the subsistence economy. Their parents, Raúl and Elena, were born several years before contact and grew up deep in the rainforest. "Matses people didn't use money back then!" they recount, and having learned how to provide food from a very young age, they now urge their children to do the same. But the boys are also developing desires, hopes, and aspirations for the future that break with the kind of persons their parents are and represent an active choice to become new kinds of economic agents—first and foremost, becoming able to make money and enjoy the opportunities afforded by the market economy, as suggested by my dialogue below with Diego.

DIEGO: When I'm older, I will travel abroad.

CAMILLA: Where will you go?

DIEGO: Where the *chotac* live. Iquitos, Lima. And maybe your country!

CAMILLA: What would you like to do there?

DIEGO: See what the people there are like [*matses ushu issec*, literally, "Look at the white people"]. And buy things.

CAMILLA: What will you buy?

DIEGO: Clothes! A lot of clothes, and shoes. New shoes.

This is one among countless instances of children telling me that in the future they want to make money to travel and buy manufactured goods, especially clothes such as T-shirts, long trousers, and trainers. Diego and Mateo wear old, stained clothes and shoes ruined by the weather, or cheap flip-flops that break easily, and they do not own many goods of their own, such as flashlights and the small knives that Matses children desire. They spend about a month every year with their parents in Colonia Angamos, but neither of them has ever traveled to the nearest city, Iquitos, which is much farther afield. Their parents, who wouldn't be able to afford to pay for their travel expenses, have rarely been there themselves, but they are not so concerned about the city and do not share their children's fascination with the outside world and *chotac* people.

This is not to say that older generations of Matses are not interested in money or manufactured goods or desire these less than children do. Subsistence activities are now entwined with the use of cash, which is perceived as a scarce though increasingly necessary resource by all generations and which Diego and

Mateo's parents mainly access by selling plantain, manioc, and other agricultural products on their sporadic visits to town, or by taking part in Enrique's genipap juice business, none of these being particularly fruitful. Back in the 1990s, when he was already an adult and Matses interactions with *chotac* people had started to increase, Diego and Mateo's father, Raúl, moved temporarily to Colonia Angamos to work as a builder. "I wanted to buy machetes," he recounts to explain his desire to make money, but he recalls this as a wearisome and unpleasant experience. He hated living in town and having to deal with the *chotac*, and after being paid he quickly squandered his wages without saving any money, in a way that is all too common among older Matses men who have worked in the wage economy of the *chotac* world.

Managing money requires skills, such as saving and frugality, which stand in clear contrast to the attitude of the hunter and his family, who consume meat quickly and are proud to share with others if their catch is abundant. Despite being unsuccessful in town, Raúl was happy to return to his village in the forest, where he can continue to engage in the everyday practices that for him are not only a necessity but something that makes life meaningful: hunting, trekking, foraging, working in the fields, and so forth. While he and his wife complain that there's no money and they are only rarely able to buy cartridges, fishing tools, or clothes for their children, they nevertheless prefer to remain close to the rainforest and continue to engage in traditional subsistence activities.

Diego and Mateo, on the other hand, work hard in the household economy but do not share their parents' passion for the forest. They do not regard *chonuadec* (hard physical work) as highly as the older generations do, especially compared with the new kind of skills and practices they intend to master. Neither knows how to hunt, collect medicinal plants, or trek alone through the forest without getting lost—skills that their father sees as foundational to being a man—and instead, both of them told me that in the future they see themselves living in the city to *piucquid bedec* (make money). When I asked how exactly they will earn cash, they sometimes replied, "I will run a shop, like Enrique."

Halfway through my fieldwork, Mateo took part in Enrique's genipap juice business; he processed the fruits to produce ink and received a fixed wage from Enrique, which he and Diego used to set up their own little shop. They gave the money earned to their aunt, who was traveling to Iquitos, and asked her to buy some goods in the city, which they displayed in Mateo's house and sold to the other villagers. But their profits were low and their shop was soon shut down, as I mentioned, and Mateo said to me: "I'd like to run a bigger store, but how can I find the money to buy more goods? There's nothing you can do here. You can work for Enrique sometimes, but that's it. There's no work in the village. There's no money. When I'm older, I want to work in Angamos or Iquitos, so that I can buy things for myself."

Matses children and teenagers are presented with different possibilities as to the adults they could become. On the one hand, Raul, Elena, and their generation, great hunters and forest dwellers who have mastered rainforest skills and trek fearlessly through the woods; and on the other, Enrique and Tito, who are not as skilled at traditional forest activities but have succeeded in the *chotac* world, especially at making money. While absent in its material form, the imagined presence of money has brought in new possibilities for the children and new desires with regard to whom they want to become and what they are striving toward, where money-making appears as a more flavorsome alternative compared with the path trodden by previous generations.

Marketing the Spirits: Children's Aspirations for the Future

At the age of thirteen, Leonora is an active economic agent and a food provider who fully contributes to household subsistence through fishing, working in the family's field, cleaning the house, washing clothes and plates, fetching water, looking after younger siblings, and so forth. But like all children and teenagers, Leonora is also aspiring to attain a different adulthood from that of her mother, and part of this means accessing the monetary economy. While money-making is perceived as primarily a male activity, Leonora also tried to earn cash herself by processing the genipap juice for Enrique, like Diego's older brother Mateo, and she once asked me to take a photograph of her holding a machete and a fruit from the genipap tree, her hands stained from touching the fruit and making the juice (figure 18).

Leonora's mother, Manola, grew up in the rainforest before contact and also processed genipap fruits at around the same age. But unlike her daughter, Manola did it to produce the black ink that Matses people used to create permanent body tattoos, which, as explained in chapter 1, was a fundamental rite of passage that turned a child into a real *matses*, literally "person," as well as a practice through which older generations nourished a social relationship with the forest and its nonhuman inhabitants. For Manola's generation, tattooing was entwined with a moral economy based on hunting practices and predicated on animistic values, where sustenance was based on mutual exchanges with the forest world.

Leonora refused the tattoo, like all teenagers—and when I asked her and other young people why, they always answered, "*issatsquio nec*" (The tattoo is ugly). Not only does she not share the desire to distinguish her body from those of *chotac* people; most girls of the same age even regard the *chotac* body as beautiful, better looking than their own even, and both Matses boys and girls express the wish to marry a *chotac* partner in the future. In the words of Katherine Verdery, the use of money is "creating a new morality—especially a new *economic*

FIGURE 18 Leonora with genipap tree fruits (photographs by the author).

morality" (1995: 7; emphasis in original), one in which young people no longer engage—practically, emotionally, and spiritually—with the world of the forest and its inhabitants because they are gradually losing interest in it.

This is further indicated by visible differences in how children and elderly people relate to the *chëshëte*, the genipap tree used to make the tattooing ink. It is worth restating here that from a Matses perspective the *chëshëte* is not merely a tree but a powerful being owned by a *mayan*, a "forest spirit." But while elderly Matses frequently talk about forest spirits, including the *chëshëte*, as inhabitants of the nearby forest that can engage in social relations with humans, the young generations mainly associate the genipap tree with Enrique's business, and with trade.

The children themselves showed me something striking on one of our photographic group walks around the village, during which I gave them cameras and asked them to show me anything that captured their attention. As we were walking around, they casually pointed at some trees and took a photograph, simply saying, "This is the *chëshëte* they planted" (see figure 19). When I encouraged them to tell me more about the genipap and whether they thought it was dangerous to plant it near the village, the children showed little interest in the conversation, telling me, "Go ask my grandparents."

Later, their parents explained that in the past couple of years the growing demand for genipap juice from the United States has led Matses people to make

FIGURE 19 Genipap trees planted near people's houses (photograph by Celia, twelve years old).

an unprecedented decision: they planted genipap trees near their houses to speed up the process of collecting the fruits, which goes against the teachings of the *tsësiobo*, the old people, and the view of the *chëshëte* not as a tree but as a dangerous, vengeful spirit. Some of the elders initially disapproved of this decision but eventually accepted it because they too are becoming frustrated with the lack of money. Young people and children, meanwhile, seem utterly unconcerned, and they happily took me to see the trees and take photographs of them. While most Matses adults, especially the elders born before contact, still refer to the *chëshëte* as a powerful spirit, a whole new generation of children have been born into a world where genipap trees are planted near their homes, which is likely to have significant implications for their own cosmological understandings of the nonhuman world.

My aim here is not to reiterate old-fashioned theories according to which the sudden use of money in societies with nonmonetary economies "makes inanimate things reproduce and confounds categories among human, spirit, and natural worlds" (Maurer 2006: 21). Rather, I want to draw attention to how the use of money is opening up new ways of being in and understanding the world, which in this instance means creating a cosmological view where the *chëshëte* exists at once as powerful spirit and as a tree that generates cash, and thus brings into being new targets and aspirations for children's imagined adulthoods.

Like other teenagers, Leonora told me that in the future she would like to make money to buy clothes and shoes, adding that she has considered moving temporarily to Colonia Angamos to "wash clothes for the *chotac*" there, which means working as a cleaner for local *chotac* families. A few girls have done this in the past, and many of them did not have pleasant experiences: they were underpaid, did not enjoy their time there, and missed their own families. But as Leonora said, "*utsi nidebëdec*": if she wants to make money "there is no other option." At the same time as choosing money as a key goal for the future, the children are also developing an awareness of being poor and excluded from the very opportunities they hope to avail themselves of.

School and Money: A Broken Promise

The primary bridge between Matses communities and the market economy ought to be school education, which Matses people understand as necessary to provide children with the skills and knowledge to succeed in the *chotac* world—first and foremost accessing waged jobs. When I asked why schooling is necessary, children and adults replied that school helps the children learn basic skills such as reading, writing, and mathematics, which will help them deal with the *chotac* and do business with them when they are older. As Andres, a thirty-two-year-old father of four, once told me, "If my children sell plantains to the *chotac* they must know how much they weigh. If they don't know that this sack of plantains weighs two kilos, the *chotac* will tell them: this is one kilo! and give them less money for it. Or if the *chotac* cheat and underpay them my children will not realize it, if they don't know how to count money."

The connection between school education and economic development is an explicit part of Peruvian state policies; indeed, enhancing school programs in rural areas is presented as a key governmental strategy to reduce the dramatic levels of poverty affecting the country, where "schooling is considered to be a key means of bringing about modernization and economic development" (Aikman 2002: 41; see also Rockwell and Gomes 2009). But as elsewhere in the world, school education in Peru is predicated on radical inequalities, where recent and ongoing forms of privatization are leading to what Patricia Ames calls "educational segregation" (2021): a system that affords pupils from low-income, rural, and Indigenous backgrounds much-reduced educational opportunities and substantially lower standards of schooling.

Consequently, both in Amazonia and elsewhere across the world, school programs promoted by the state often fail to impart Indigenous and hunter-gatherer children with satisfactory academic knowledge, while at the same time distancing them from the knowledge and skills of their elders (Anderson-Levitt

2005; Lancy 2010, 2012b; Morelli 2013; Rogoff et al. 2003). In Peru, a number of anthropologists and Indigenous activists have sought to address this educational failure by working together to promote bilingual and intercultural curriculums that can help children access the opportunities offered by national society, while also respecting their own worldviews and cultural approaches to learning (Aikman 2002; Gasché 2004; Trapnell 2009).

In Matses society, the best possible prospect schooling can open is that of becoming a schoolteacher, the most lucrative type of job for a Matses person. Most parents in the village told me that their hope is for their children to become teachers in the future, but this is not an easy path. Working as a schoolteacher requires completing secondary school in the village and then studying at the university in Iquitos, which is very costly. And whereas the first generation of teachers, including Enrique and Tito, were supported by the missionaries and received training as part of a governmental program of school introduction in Indigenous communities, students are now expected to find their own means to complete their degree. The Ministry of Education offers some scholarships for Indigenous students, but these are few and far between, and the majority of young Matses who study to become schoolteachers are funded by their parents. And since the costs of living in Iquitos are so high, the only families who can afford to support their children are those of schoolteachers themselves. In many cases, schoolteachers pay for their children to specialize in Iquitos even if they are not talented students, causing some resentment among other families.

Matses children are aware that the benefits of school education cannot be fully achieved if they are not supported by economic wealth, and since most perceive themselves as poor, the children seem not to expect much from schooling—not even the more talented pupils. One of these talented students is Diego, the teenager who opened a shop with his brother. The teachers told me that Diego is an exceptionally good student, and I often noticed myself how quick and clever he was. But when I asked him whether he intends to study in Iquitos and work as a schoolteacher, Diego told me that his parents wouldn't be able to support him and that he will have to find alternative ways of making money.

For the Matses, as well as other hunter-gatherer and rural peoples across the world, the introduction of state schooling seems to leave children with limited skills and resources for entering the national society, while having "made more people aware of how 'poor' they were, of how many wondrous things they lacked the cash to purchase" (Lancy 1996: 199). As I discussed, elderly Matses recount that there was no such thing as having no money when they were children and lived itinerantly through hunting, gathering, and horticulture, owning no manufactured goods apart from old machetes and shotguns they stole through raiding and shared with each other, and that therefore they knew no individual differentiations based on material or monetary wealth.

The idea of being poor is entwined with the recent and growing reliance on manufactured goods, money, and trading bonds with the *chotac* and ultimately with Matses livelihoods becoming increasingly entangled with national and global economies. This is creating a growing predicament for the Matses, who have to reconcile this reliance on the market economy with both a geographical distance and a lack of resources that separate them from it, having limited means to benefit from the very economic structures they are coming to rely on. The same kind of economic hardship and marginality is experienced by Indigenous people worldwide, who are estimated to constitute 6 percent of the world's population but 19 percent of the world's poor (Dhir et al. 2019).

Matses children are not simply caught up in this process but playing a dynamic role within it. Money is a crucial part of the world as they know it, as suggested by Diego, Edgar, and other boys who admitted their desire to make money when they grow up, as well as by Leonora and other girls who express the desire to work for *chotac* families. By becoming affectively and emotionally attached to money—and the lifestyles money can afford—the children are projecting themselves toward new horizons and setting up the conditions for new economic futures, much like they are driving a transition toward riverine livelihoods and fishing economies by becoming affectively attached to the river. As such, their desire for cash and progressive disengagement with the traditional subsistence economy is a purposeful and revolutionary action leading to deep social and economic change.

4

Consuelo's Dolls

Shifting Desires and the Subversion of Womanhood

CAMILLA: Who are these?

CONSUELO: My dolls.

CAMILLA: Are these Matses women?

CONSUELO: No! These are *chotac* women.

CAMILLA: I see. What do they do? Are they *dayac* [hardworking]?

CONSUELO: No, they aren't *dayac*. They eat bread, and they watch television all day. [See figure 20.]

I have shown that children's cravings for new lifestyles and shifting desires between the generations are driving radical change, channeling the course of social life toward new and untested futures. This process has gendered dimensions. As new economic opportunities arise, traditional subsistence activities are replaced, and environmental relationships transform through time, children and teenagers are beginning to question the choices and moral values of their elders, while developing new understandings of how to be a gendered person and to behave as such.

This includes changing ideas and understandings of what it means to be a *chido*, a "woman," and to become one. Matses girls and young women are faced with multiple and conflicting images of womanhood: their grandmothers, who grew up in the deep rainforest before contact and emphasize the value of working hard within the household economy; their mothers and other younger Matses women, who continue to work hard but are also developing new desires, such as moving closer to town and accessing the market economy; and *chotac* women who live in the city and embody a radically different kind of womanhood.

FIGURE 20 Consuelo's dolls (photograph by Lily, nine years old).

In classic anthropological literature, Amazonian women have often been portrayed as "the passive element of culture, sometimes appearing as a circulating currency between factions to guarantee alliances based on kinship" (Vinente dos Santos 2012: 97; my translation). Latin American and Indigenous feminist scholars have been challenging this representation, grounded in a colonialist male gaze, and emphasized the multifaceted and dynamic forms of resistance against patriarchal, colonial structures of power and exploitation (Gargallo 2006: 154–174; Segato 2014). Here I follow their lead as I attempt to propose an analysis that centers the voices, perspectives, and experiences of Matses girls and young women, highlighting their dynamic agency in ongoing processes of social transformation. Through an in-depth ethnographic account based on our interactions in the field, I explore how Matses girls are developing subversive desires and new expectations of womanhood, undermining traditional gendered norms and opening up new pathways for being and becoming a woman.[1]

Being *Dayac* Is Women's Nature

Consuelo is six years old and tiny, but capable of conducting demanding work such as carrying a big pile of pots and pans to the river and washing it all by herself (figure 21). Similarly to boys who should become *dadambo* (very manly)

FIGURE 21 Consuelo washes up pots and pans in the river (photography by Elsie, nine years old).

from a young age, girls are actively encouraged to develop skills and engage in forms of labor that will make them *dayac*, "hard-working" and inclined to conduct the demanding activities required daily by the household economy.

The value of being *dayac* runs through different generations of women and is seen as constitutive of womanhood—as Matses people say, being *dayac* is *chidobon padibi*, meaning "women's nature," as can be observed in the hard labor performed daily by all women in Matses villages. Like all the other girls, every day Consuelo helps her twenty-one-year-old mother, Dalila, and her grandmother Ivana, who lives in the same household, with a range of household activities such as cooking, washing up, cleaning, and looking after younger siblings. While a young girl carrying a bowl full of pots and pans from her house to the creek and washing it by herself clashes with the idea of "children as vulnerable cherubs" widespread in industrialized societies (Lancy 2008), it is a common sight in Matses villages, where girls even younger than Consuelo carry out challenging physical tasks on a daily basis.

This everyday behavior can be interpreted as what Judith Butler called performative or "stylized" acts through which a certain idea of gender is established and assumed as natural (1990: 179). Butler questioned the view that sex is a material or biological fact given at birth and that gender is constructed subjectively or culturally upon that material ground. Instead, she proposed that "gender is an identity tenuously constituted in time, instituted in an exterior space through a *stylized repetition of acts*" (179; emphasis in original). In other words, someone who has been told from birth that she is a *woman* will (albeit unknowingly) reproduce the ways of acting, walking, and talking of the other people she sees around her who were also told to be *women*.

By emulating these stylized and repetitive acts, these subjects in turn put out in the world an idea that there is something naturally, objectively, or biologically true that we can call "women" and who are thus seen as sharing some kind of inner womanly core that produces the kinds of behavior in which most members of the group "women" appear to engage; whereas in fact this behavior is instilled through repetition and imitation, even if people may not be aware of doing it—it is *performative*. In Butler's words, "the action of gender requires a performance that is repeated," and this "repetition is at once a re-enactment and re-experiencing of a set of meanings already socially established" (1990: 178). The hard work carried out daily by Matses women can be seen as one of those stylized, repetitive acts through which an idea of the naturally female is created; in this case, the idea that being *dayac* is women's nature.

This is not to say that the will to work hard is seen as arising spontaneously in girls. As I described earlier, child-rearing is seen as a purposeful act of making where parents must push their children to develop appropriate qualities and ways of behaving, and this includes pushing their daughters to becomes *dayac* and not be lazy, which is a shameful and much-reprimanded quality for Matses people, especially the elderly. At the age of six, Consuelo has already developed a strong *dayac* ethic, and when plates need to be washed or water fetched from the river, she is likely to do so without her mother needing to ask. But if her mother does ask for help, for example by asking her daughter to accompany her to the cultivated field and help carry back harvested manioc or plantains, Consuelo is unlikely to refuse. If she does, her mother will tell her off or make fun of her, calling her *uspu* (lazy), which will soon push Consuelo to go and work.

Elderly people occasionally force girls to take frog poison, which as I described earlier transmits *sinan*, a kind of energy that is at once material and spiritual. If transmitted to a boy, *sinan* stimulates his growth into a *dadambo* man, while if transmitted to a girl it helps her develop *dayac* qualities and a will to work hard, as Consuelo told me.

CONSUELO: My grandad made me take the poison a while ago.

CAMILLA: Oh yes? Did you enjoy it?

CONSUELO: No! I was very scared. He grabbed me by the arm and put poison on it. And then, *buah!* I threw up! [laughs].

CAMILLA: Why did he give the poison to you?

CONSUELO: So that I become *dayac!* Like my grandmother.

CAMILLA: Is your grandmother *dayac*?

CONSUELO: Yes! She's very *dayac*. She has taken a lot of frog poison.

Consuelo's grandmother Ivana is a *macho*, an "elderly woman" born before contact and unsure of her exact age. She is the first wife of Julio, my adoptive brother, whom I introduced earlier. Matses people are polygynous, meaning that men can have multiple wives, and like most men of his generation, Julio has two and lives with the younger one, while Ivana lives in the same house as her daughter Dalila, her daughter's husband, Hernán, and their two children, Consuelo and Kenny.

Ivana is the epitome of *dayac*: she works for hours every day in the cultivated field, planting and harvesting manioc and plantain in the overpowering Amazonian heat, and she also goes fishing and harvesting wild fruit, berries, and firewood in the forest. Unlike women from younger generations, she knows how to craft hammocks using forest vines and make small pots using river clay, and knows where to find wild honey, berries, and other forest goods. Having grown up in deep rainforest, Ivana can move confidently among the thick vegetation, trekking long distances by herself without getting lost or scared, whereas her daughter Dalila will not walk through the forest alone, and her granddaughter Consuelo, like the rest of the children, barely treks at all.

Ivana told me that she became *dayac* herself when she was as small as Consuelo, by engaging in the same, if not even more, hardworking behavior, as she recounts: "When I was a child, we didn't have machetes like we do now, Camilla! We only had some old, rusty ones that the men stole from the chotac when they raided them. But those machetes were no good, and we had to work with our hands in the field, digging soil [mimics the act of digging soil with one hand]. It was very, very hard. I helped my mother every day to plant and harvest plantains and manioc. The skin on my hands was thick and hard [laughs]. I was a *dayac* girl."

For Ivana and her generation, becoming *dayac* meant not only developing skills that are necessary to the functioning of the social economy but also growing into a sexually appealing woman, just as being *dadambo* and a good hunter is seen as making a man attractive. Ivana recounts that Julio felt attracted to her for being so *dayac*, and the sex appeal of a woman who is hardworking and industrious can still be seen in the attitude and behavior of elderly men. Once, a group of Matses men aged between forty and sixty came to visit the village where I was working and had dinner with Julio and Serena's family. Nancy, their fifteen-year-old daughter, prepared dinner for all the guests: she lit the fire, cooked the food, served it to the guests, and then cleaned the house and prepared to go to the river to wash the plates, all on her own. As she handed out to each of them a plate full of food, the men exploded with loud whistles of admiration, howling, "Look at you, Nancy, you are *dayac*!" in a playful tone that still revealed true appreciation.

This sexual desire for a *dayac* woman is inherently linked to the economy of hunting that Matses people used to practice when they lived in deep rainforest (and to a lesser extent still practice today) which is predicated on reciprocal exchanges between the married couple, where women primarily contribute to subsistence through harvesting the fields and cooking food, and men by providing meat. For Ivana and Julio's generation, the tasks that make a woman *dayac*—cooking, washing, cleaning, cultivating the field, and carrying products—are seen as complementary to the tasks that make a man *dadambo*, first and foremost that of providing protein through hunting. Elderly Matses make this explicit when recounting how they got married in the past. The term I am translating as "getting married" is *chido bedec*, literally "to take a wife." People say that a man *takes* a woman as his *chido* (wife), and occasionally they can say that a woman *takes* a man as her *bënë* (husband), but this is a much less common expression. Matses people do not perform any specific marriage ritual, but a man and a woman are called husband and wife when they build a house of their own and start having children—and the elderly people recount that when they were young, a man had to prove his hunting skills to the woman's family, and particularly to his mother-in-law, in order to get married.

When Julio decided to take Ivana, he moved into the house where she lived with her family and, for a few weeks, he went hunting every day and brought back meat, which he handed to Ivana's mother. Ivana recalls this with pride, saying that Julio caught so much they could feed the whole family with it. Julio's skill as a hunter impressed her family, who agreed for him to take Ivana, at which point he built a house for the two of them, sanctioning their married status. Classic structuralist works have argued that this kind of reciprocity is constitutive of marital relationships in Amazonia, where the exchanges between wife and husband are essential to the functioning of the subsistence economy; and given that the entire social structure of Indigenous Amazonian societies is founded upon this economy, the married couple and the division of labor between them are at the very core to the organization of society as a whole (see Walker 2013).

Consuelo performing hard work every day shows a degree of continuity in the construction of womanhood between the generations, where the longitudinal repetition of these acts in time reinforces an idea of *dayac*-ness being women's nature. But while ideas of gender are reproduced through repeated action, they can also be radically subverted—where *subversive acts* are understood as a kind of behavior that diverts from what is seen as natural or normal and, as such, challenges established assumptions about the very nature of gender. Subversive acts are "a failure to repeat, a deformity . . . that exposes the phantasmatic effect of abiding identity as a politically tenuous construction" (Butler 1990: 214), opening up the possibility for gender norms to be questioned and radically destabilized.

Consuelo told me that her main desires for the future are to have money, to buy clothes, and to travel to the city, Iquitos, where she will be able to watch television and eat city food such as rice and sugar. So while she is to an extent reenacting established gendered behaviors, she is also developing new aspirations that challenge them. Crucially, Consuelo wants a different kind of husband: no longer a skilled hunter, like her grandfather Julio, but a money-maker who will contribute to the household economy by bringing in cash, as shown in our dialogue below.

CONSUELO: Are you married, Camilla?

CAMILLA: No, I'm not.

CONSUELO: Do you have a boyfriend?

CAMILLA: No, I don't—do you?

CONSUELO: No, I don't. [Pauses.] Who would you like to marry: a Matses man, or a *chotac* man?

CAMILLA: I don't know! How about you?

CONSUELO: [Whispers.] A *chotac*.

CAMILLA: Really? Why would you like to marry a *chotac*?

CONSUELO: Because he'll give me clothes.

CAMILLA: And Matses men? Can't they buy you clothes?

CONSUELO: No! Matses men haven't got any money.

The dialogue reported above is one among many initiated by girls who told me that *chotac* men are more desirable and they *daschute menec* (give clothes) to their wives, whereas I never heard a girl mention hunting and the ability to provide meat as desirable qualities in a husband. Consuelo *bunec* (desires) a man who is a *chotac* outsider and a money-maker, and she does not care for hunting skills. She covets a lifestyle that is different from her grandmother's, one where she has money, buys clothes, and spends time in the city instead of crafting hammocks and pots or looking for medicinal plants in the forest. The consequences of these shifting desires can already be seen in the households of young women in their late teens or early twenties, who grew up in sedentary villages along the riverbank and never developed a passion for the forest.

Damita: Desire as a Subversive Act

DAMITA: Why aren't you married, Camilla?

CAMILLA: I don't know! I guess I haven't met the right person.

DAMITA: I see. [Pauses.] You shouldn't marry someone you don't want!

CAMILLA: Did you want Fabián, when he took you?

DAMITA: No, I didn't! I used to bite his hands when he tried to touch me. [We both laugh.]

CAMILLA: How old were you?

DAMITA: I was only thirteen when he took me. My brother gave me to him in exchange for Fabián's sister. I was just a child, Camilla. I was exchanged. I was stupid; I didn't have a clue.

CAMILLA: But now you do want Fabián?

DAMITA: Yes, now I do.

CAMILLA: Will Paula be exchanged? [I point at her three-year-old daughter, who is sitting in the room with us.]

DAMITA: No, I wouldn't like her to be exchanged. Paula should be married to a man she wants. [Then she smiles, comes closer to me, and whispers, as if someone could hear us although we are alone,] I'd like her husband to be a *chotac*.

CAMILLA: You'd like Paula to be with a *chotac*?!

DAMITA: [Still whispering.] Yes, if she wants.

CAMILLA: Why?

DAMITA: For the clothes! And the money, too.

Damita is twenty-two years old and has been married for nine years to Fabián, who is twenty-seven. In the kinship system of Matses people, classified as Dravidian, Damita and Fabián are what anthropologists term "cross-cousins," denoting the offspring of the father's sisters or the offspring of the mother's brothers; in this case, Damita's father and Fabián's mother are siblings, which makes Damita and Fabián cross-cousins. In this kinship system, a prescriptive marriage rule establishes that sexual relationships and marriage are only allowed between cross-cousins, and while sexual intercourse between cross-cousins is free and common, including through extramarital affairs, intercourse with anybody else not classified as a cross-cousin is considered incest, and is strictly forbidden.[2]

Damita and Fabián have three other children besides Paula: John (ten), Harry (eight), and Erik (two). I lived with them for a month during my fieldwork, and every day I witnessed Damita's *dayac*-ness expressed in her ability to provide for all her children with her strenuous work. During the first two weeks I lived with them, Fabián was in Iquitos, and Damita carried out most of the housework, with some help from John and Harry, Paula's older brothers. She woke up early in the morning to set out to cultivate and harvest the field, carrying back heavy loads of manioc, plantains, and papayas on her head. Next she went fishing and was able to provide enough fish for herself and her four children.

Then she prepared food, cleaned the house, and washed clothes and plates. Although I always sought to help, I could never keep up with Damita, and my main contributions to the household were through manufactured goods and food that I had brought from the city: rice, salt, sugar, and cooking oil—which made the children incredibly happy to have me around—and also gasoline to enable us to go fishing on the Yaquerana River, where fish are more abundant.

For Damita, being a mother and being *dayac* are entangled and form the very essence of womanhood. She often expressed disbelief that, being in my mid-twenties, as I was when we first met, I was still unmarried and had no children. For her, being a mother is not just a choice but something that is perceived as inseparable from being a woman—in Matses society, across the generations, being a mother is understood as part of women's nature, and becoming a mother is the defining moment when girlhood turns into womanhood. Matses women were not only surprised but also saddened that I do not have children; they often remarked, without hiding their pity, that I must be living a pretty lonely and miserable life back home.

It is common for Matses women to get married at thirteen or fourteen years of age, as long as they have entered puberty, at which point they are no longer considered a child but a *buntac*, a "young woman" in her prime, reinforcing the view that the social category of childhood is constructed and negotiated differently across cultural contexts. For elderly Matses, it is not only acceptable but *natural* for young teenage women to begin having children, and they often expressed that there is something not just unusual but almost unhealthy in a woman such as myself who remains unmarried and childless through her twenties. They often said, "You know, Camilla, if you don't get married and have children soon, nobody will want you anymore!"

Damita expressed the same disbelief, but her generation has started questioning whether women should have children in their early teens. She talks bitterly about having had to do so against her own will, and says that she "didn't have a clue" when Fabián took her, because she was "just a child" and too young to take a stand against it. Since Matses people are virilocal (i.e., a woman is expected to move to her husband's village after marriage), Damita had to leave her family when her husband took her and move to his village, and she still recalls the deep sorrow of missing her mother. "I cried a lot," she told me; "I really missed my mother and since I've moved to this village, I barely see her." At the time, Fabián was nineteen years old, and he neither asked for nor considered Damita's opinion and simply made a deal with Damita's brother, following a new marriage rule that emerged in the years after missionary contact: that of sister exchange.

This new marriage practice began when Matses society entered the transition from a forest-based hunting economy toward riverine livelihoods, which meant that hunting was no longer the primary subsistence activity. Because men were no longer as skilled at hunting, they would not seek marriage approval from their in-laws by providing meat and instead began performing a form of exchange where two young men make an agreement to marry each other's sisters. In this case, Damita's brother met Fabián's sister, and they decided to settle down and have children. But in order for the union to be approved, Damita's brother had to give his own sister, Damita, in exchange to his wife's brother, Fabián. The Matses explain this as a mechanism that ensures a wife for every man, and because Matses couples have many children, it is unlikely that a man will have no sister to exchange. As commonly happens in sister-exchange, one couple mutually agree to the union, but with regard to matching the other couple, only the man agrees to the exchange that secures him a wife, as happened in the case of Damita and Fabián.

Initially Damita would resist or bite Fabián's hands whenever he tried to touch her, but eventually, she says, *quenenobi*—an expression that can be translated both as "I got used to him" or "I fell in love with him." Anthropologists have long shown that the understandings and experiences of love (and, indeed, the very notion that something we can call "love" exists) are far from universal but are rather culturally constructed. For me, as I find myself saying to Damita, the idea of love that could potentially lead to marriage is about meeting the "right person" and deciding that person is good enough to spend at least a considerable amount of time with. But for Matses people, falling in love happens over time by becoming used to someone, suggesting that one *grows to love* or better *to want* someone else over time and not always following one's own choice. Damita says that now she *bunec*, truly "desires" or "loves" Fabián, and she has a deeply satisfied and fulfilled relationship with a partner she did not choose.

But Damita now wants her own daughter, Paula, to marry a man whom she *bunec*, rather than getting used to one who will take her against her will—possibly a *chotac*, an outsider who will provide for Paula through money-making, reinforcing the contrast with the desire of previous generations. She also told me that a few years back, Fabián had an affair with his unmarried cross-cousin, who became pregnant, and he suggested taking her as his second wife. Fabián's own father, Leandro, was born and grew up before contact and had two wives because, as he says himself, he was a great hunter, and to this day he can still feed both of his families. Fabián's mother, Lorena, still recalls with a certain bitterness the moment when Leandro decided to take Alina, his second wife: "When Leandro decided to marry Alina, I got mad at him. I yelled, 'No, don't take her!' But he took her anyway. I got mad, at first. But in the end, I got used to it. You know, my own father had *eight* wives. Eight!"

The now elderly women were expected to accept a co-wife, even if they were unhappy with it, as long as the man kept providing meat for his wives and all their children. Lorena eventually got used to it, suggesting that while women may have been dissatisfied with having co-wives, they eventually accepted it and, in most cases, became close friends with them. Indeed, the Matses term *dauid* can mean both "co-wife" and "best friend." But when Fabián suggested taking a second wife, Damita categorically refused: "I told him that if he did, I would leave him," she recounts, and Fabián desisted. Here desire, or *bunec*, itself becomes a subversive act revealing that unquestioned, taken-for-granted social rules are arbitrary and can be destabilized. Polygyny has visibly decreased through the generations, and while Lorena's own father had eight wives, I have not seen any man under thirty married to more than one woman.

On the other hand, like most men of his age, Fabián was perhaps easily dissuaded from taking on a second wife because having an extended family now requires money, and if money is always short with just one wife, it would never be enough for two. Like girls and young women, Damita has also conceived a desire for money and manufactured goods that she expects her partner to fulfill, and she expresses this to Fabián. Being exceptionally skilled at fishing, Damita is perfectly capable of feeding her whole family through both protein and field crops, as she demonstrated while Fabián was away. But as she told me, she hopes that Paula will marry a *chotac* because, like other women, she has also developed a new view of marital reciprocity where, ideally, a husband can provide through money-making.

A couple of weeks after I moved into their house, Fabián returned from the city, and that night he went hunting and caught a *tambis*, or lowland paca, a large rodent. Born in the early 1980s, when Matses people had only recently settled down along navigable rivers, Fabián learned to hunt when he was a child, unlike his own sons who barely ever walk through the forest, and while he may not be as skilled and *dadambo* as his father, Leandro, he nevertheless knows how to catch prey animals, provided cartridges are available. A man who knows how to catch meat makes his wife and children happy and proud, and when Fabián came back holding that large rodent everybody was very excited—but not as excited as they were to see the goods that he had brought back from the city: some clothes, fishing hooks, flashlights, batteries, and even a pair of earrings. Fabián's plan was to set up a store like the one successfully run by Enrique, and while he had also brought a few gifts for his children, including a skirt for Paula, most of the goods were to be saved up and sold in the store. When Paula saw the earrings, her eyes brightened, and she asked her father to give them to her; and when he said no, Paula started crying and begging, refusing to listen to his explanations that they needed them to make money. As we all ate rodent meat around the fire, Paula sat in a corner and spent the evening crying for the earrings.

In the following days, Fabián and I had long chats in which money kept coming up as a topic of conversation, one that clearly concerned him very much, particularly in relation to the costs of having children.

FABIÁN: Do you have children, Camilla?

CAMILLA: No, I don't!

FABIÁN: And how do you take care of that? [*midapaden cuidauaicnec*, i.e., "What contraceptive method do you use?"].

CAMILLA: I use a pill. Why is that?

FABIÁN: Could you bring some for Damita?

CAMILLA: A contraceptive pill?! Don't you want more children?

FABIÁN: No! When you have children, you need a lot of money.

CAMILLA: Why? What do you need money for?

FABIÁN: To buy them clothes. And medicines. And shoes. You need a lot of money if you have children. When I was a child, we didn't need much. Nobody had money. But now if you have kids, you need a lot of it. My children want me to buy things for them. And Damita wants me to buy clothes for her too.

Damita listened without saying a word. While Fabián was away, she had told me that she wants to have more children in the future, and no Matses woman ever asked me for contraceptive pills like this. As they say themselves, motherhood is not just rewarding but constitutive of the very nature of being a woman; but since money-making is a male activity, the pressure to earn cash falls primarily on men. As twenty-three-year-old José Antonio once said to me, "In the past, when the Matses were un-contacted, people ate a lot of sloth meat. They loved sloth meat. That was one of their favorite foods. And when a hunter caught a sloth, all the girls came running to him! [draws his hand together from far apart, to convey the idea of girls crowding up around the hunter]. It's the same as girls do now, when a guy has got money!" And while putting new forms of pressure on married men, the desire to make money is also leading to unprecedented issues for young women.

Remedios: Single Motherhood and the Subversion of Women's Nature

Remedios is seventeen years old, and everybody in the village calls her *bëda-patse*, "very pretty." She has thick, dark hair that runs the length of her back, dark skin, and a toned, Amazon-like physique, and she carries herself confidently when she walks. When I arrived in the village, Remedios had just given birth to her first child, Tatiana. She told me that the father of her baby is Santiago, her cross-cousin and the son of a schoolteacher, with whom she had started a relationship two years before. "I wanted him" she told me. "He's handsome and he would come and look for me at night, when everybody was asleep, and tell me that I'm beautiful and that he wanted me. We started having sex. He said he would marry me."

Remedios became pregnant and, shortly after, Santiago traveled to the city to look for work, as a few young men have started to do in recent years. "He said that he would build a house for us when he got back," says Remedios. But Santiago did not come back, and months later, when Remedios's daughter was born, news came from the city that he had married a *chotac* woman there and he was bringing her back to the village. Remedios suddenly found herself a single mother still living with her elderly parents.

In the everyday conversations of the young people, Santiago became a kind of superstar. A *chotac* partner is a sign of great prestige for the younger generations, and I heard several young men openly wishing to find a *chotac* woman "like Santiago did." A few months after the birth of Tatiana, while I was there conducting fieldwork, Santiago came back to the village and brought with him his *chotac* wife, Jenny, a fifteen-year-old girl from Iquitos. People in the village had been impatient to see her, and when she finally arrived, everybody commented on how attractive she looked, including Remedios. They said that Jenny is *bëdaptasë* (beautiful) because she is plump and has a big bum, bright skin, and a "doll face," features that young Matses see as signs of beauty and contrast with the slender, toned, and dark-skinned Amazon body of Matses women like Remedios.

Remedios was hurt and disappointed. She would have sudden outbursts of anger, scolding the dogs or yelling at her daughter, and she gossiped often about Santiago's *chotac* wife. She pointed out that Jenny can be plump because she is lazy, unlike most Matses women, who develop muscular, toned bodies by working hard every day in the field, in the river, and at home. "She looks like that because she doesn't do anything all day. She doesn't know how to cook, she never cleans, and she's never worked in a field her whole life. Her mother cooks for her and they buy food with money, and all she does is lie on a hammock all day! I started helping my mother when I was this big," she sticks her hand out to indicate the height of a very small child, reinforcing that, like all Matses girls, Remedios started actively contributing to the household economy early through hard physical labor.

In Remedios's view, the differences between her body and Jenny's are not just a matter of appearance, but they become the material expression of two contrasting possibilities of being a woman. Feminist anthropologist Henrietta Moore uses the term "embodied intersubjectivity" to define a context of interactions, situations, and experiences "where bodies marked through the social, that is, by difference (race, gender, ethnicity and so on) are presented as part of identities" (1994: 3). When Remedios faces Jenny, the *chotac* woman Santiago left her for, she enters a field of embodied intersubjectivity where she must confront herself with the image of a new female body—the plump, brighter-skinned, and beautiful body of a *chotac* woman, which is seen as the physical outcome of a radically different female identity informed by contrasting economic and social factors.

FIGURE 22 Matilda walks like a *chotac* woman (still from a video taken by the author).

In this encounter, Remedios's Amazon-like physique becomes the embodiment of the *dayac*-ness that is Matses women's nature, the physical expression of the daily hard work required by the subsistence economy in which women have traditionally found fulfillment by partaking in reciprocal exchanges with their hunting husbands. By contrast, Jenny's plump, *chotac* body is the product of the affordances of urban life and a market-based economy of consumption, where girls can afford not to work and are provided for by their parents.

I once filmed Matilda, a ten-year-old girl, as she was mocking *chotac* women's way of walking, while a group of other girls watch and laugh loudly (figure 22 is a still from the video). Matilda is seen swaying her hips dramatically as she steps ahead, placing one foot in front of the other and swinging her lower arms exaggeratingly along her body, like a model on a catwalk, to mimic the flirta-tious walks of *chotac* women whom she occasionally sees when traveling to Colonia Angamos. I asked Matilda and the girls around us whether they think that *chotac* women walk that way, and they replied, "Of course they do! *Aton padibi nec* [it's their nature]."

The hip-swaying, arm-swinging walk of *chotac* women stands in contrast to the straight, balanced way of walking of Matses women and girls who, like ath-letes, can run across logs placed over high cliffs in the rainforest or along the thin edge of a moving canoe. Both ways of moving can be interpreted as those *stylized repetitions of acts* theorized by Judith Butler, acts that come to be under-stood as the outcome of a womanly inner core, or in the girls' own words, as women's "nature": the *dayac*, hardworking core of Matses women on one side and the flirtatious, languid femininity of the *chotac* on the other.

Elderly people very much agree with this view: the *chotac* body is the quin-tessential expression of the lack of *dayac*-ness, for as they often say, being *dayac* is not the nature of *chotac* women, who are lazy and clumsy and cannot work hard. For them, this makes *chotac* people unattractive and undesirable. A woman swaying her hips or batting her eyelashes has no particular grasp on elderly Mat-ses men, who are not just critical of but actively displeased and put off by *chotac* laziness. One day, Remedios started talking about Jenny being lazy and the fact that Santiago desired her. Her elderly grandfather Isaías, who was nearby, over-heard us and asked, bemused, "Why would anyone want to have sex with a lazy woman?," reinforcing that, as I have said, for elderly Matses a *dayac* woman is not just a reliable companion in the household economy but also sexy.

The younger generations do not share this view. They no longer perceive lazi-ness as off-putting but attractive—it is part of the appeal of the *chotac* world, where young people have money and can use it to live, watch television during the day instead of working in a field, and lie in hammocks while their parents buy food for them. If *chotac* women are clumsier, weaker, and quickly tire of work-ing, this is not an issue for them, especially because *chotac* women have differ-ent skills. I once asked a young man who had a short affair with a woman in the city why the *chotac* are so desirable. In addition to the usual answer "Because they are pretty," the young man replied, "Because they kiss." Matses people do not kiss each other, and while the elderly find kissing rather repulsive, especially if done in public, young Matses are fascinated by it. I asked the young man, "What was it like, kissing?" and he replied, "*batambo*," an adjective that recalls the taste of wild berries and papayas, or city products like sugar and candy and which trans-lates as "so sweet."

The photograph at the beginning of the chapter (figure 20) shows Consue-lo's dolls, an extremely rare commodity among Matses children. Indeed, these are the only dolls I have ever seen in the village. As Consuelo said to me, her dolls are *chotac* women who "eat bread and watch television all day," something that both girls and boys are constructing as a desirable and attractive way of being. Consuelo herself told me that in the future she wants to spend time in the city to eat bread and watch television, like her dolls do in her imagination, and a growing number of young women have started saying they are bored of working in the garden and laboring so hard; they would rather live like Consuelo's dolls, being in the city and watching television all day.

As a *chido ushu*, a "white woman," I am myself part of the world of the *chotac* and considered to have a different nature from that of Matses women—something Remedios and I often discussed when talking about our different bodies and skills. Compared with her, for instance, when paddling a canoe, trekking through the forest, or cultivating the field, I always appear big and physically unskilled. Matses people call me *chido dapa* (fat woman), emphasizing my lack of agility and skills compared with them. When I worked in the field with Remedios or other Matses women, I got tired quickly and could not carry even half of their loads, walking slowly and clumsily through the woods.

Matses elders, especially, mocked me for being ungainly and lacking many fundamental female qualities and skills, saying that the only thing I can do is work at a laptop, something they find pretty useless. For the younger generations, however, owning a laptop and being able to use it is infinitely more attractive and a more valuable skill than planting and harvesting a field. So while I am in many ways a strange kind of woman—unmarried, childless, very tall, and unable to conduct activities that even six-year-olds can do with ease—I also have many desirable qualities, in terms of skills, such as laptop use, and even physical appearance. Remedios and others in the village often called me fat and pointed out that I have a "big bum," hinting that my body is also afforded by my own economic possibilities, as shown by the following dialogue.

REMEDIOS: When you come back next time, can you bring some of your vitamins for me?

CAMILLA: Vitamins? What vitamins?

REMEDIOS: Your vitamins, to get fatter.

CAMILLA: Vitamins to get fatter?! What do you mean?

REMEDIOS: How can you get your hips so big, and your arms thin? What vitamins do you take to be like that?

CAMILLA: I don't take anything! There are no such vitamins, to get fatter.

REMEDIOS: So, you're saying that's the way you are?

CAMILLA: Yes, it is!

REMEDIOS: Sure.

Assuming that I take fattening pills, which they called *vitaminas*, to grow large hips, Remedios and other girls often asked me to buy some for them. On one occasion Leonora (the thirteen-year-old girl shown in figure 18 with the geni-pap fruits) saw me taking rehydration tablets and, thinking I was out of ear-shot, whispered to her younger sister, "Look, she's taking her vitamins." When I asked for an explanation, Leonora blushed and mumbled, "Yes, your vitamins that make you get fatter." I told Leonora, and other women, that there are no such things as hips-fattening vitamins, but they always looked unconvinced and kept asking me to buy them some.

This perceived difference between Indigenous and non-Indigenous woman-hood is charged with moral values and is affecting how women view them-selves, their bodies, and the kinds of women they are. After being confronted with Jenny, Remedios has learned to see herself as skinny, *chëshëmbo* (very dark skinned), and lacking the attractive way-of-doing of *chotac* women. She doesn't know how to kiss, she doesn't walk with a sway in her hips, and she is a *dayac* woman who works in the field and carries out domestic chores—a desirable qual-ity for elderly people, but not so for the young ones.

These shifting desires between different generations have impacts on the economy and on the future of Matses society. After Santiago left her for Jenny, Remedios became a single mother and she is now raising her baby in the house of her elderly parents, both of whom were born and grown up before contact. The elders told me that such a thing would not have happened in the past, when men had several wives and non-Matses women were taken captive through raiding. There were cases of divorce, and couples would split, but according to them, these were nowhere near as frequent as they have become in the past ten to fifteen years, since young men have started traveling to the city with greater frequency and leaving their partners even when they became pregnant, hop-ing instead to find a *chotac* woman.[3]

In subverting traditional gender values and questioning that *dayac* is the natural way to be, young Matses women are also setting themselves up for new challenges and in many ways embracing hegemonic views of womanhood that originate from the outside. Similar issues are experienced elsewhere across the world, as reported by a number of Indigenous feminist scholars who offer inter-pretative frameworks of resistance against the colonialist power structures affecting Indigenous women's lives (Simpson 2009; Suzack et al. 2010). In response to this, all across Latin America a rising number of activists and women-run organizations are seeking to improve the lives of Indigenous girls and women according to culturally specific values and ideas of gender (Black-well 2012; Sempértegui 2019).

These issues are still new for the Matses, given their extremely recent his-tory of contact with outside society, but a few young women have already started voicing their concerns with regard to the difficulties experienced by their gen-eration. On my last visit to Peru, I heard for the first time a few young women who have migrated to the city discuss the gender-specific challenges they face and stressing the need for educational programs that will help girls in the community to achieve better futures. They mentioned promoting women-run programs of reforestation, delivering family-planning education for girls in rural villages, and setting up initiatives that can generate fair sources of income for women in rural communities without them having to rely on their husbands to earn cash. While these narratives have only just begun to emerge among Matses women, they nevertheless gesture toward new forms of resistance and empowerment driven by young women themselves.

5

Jean-Claude Van Damme in the Rainforest

The Spoken Weapons of Masculinity

CRISTIANO: Bat ears!

CLARITA: Spider anus!

CRISTIANO: Forest spirit's husband!

CLARITA: River dolphin's husband!

CRISTIANO: River dolphin nose!

CLARITA: Tapir nose!

[I walk toward the children and they see me.]

CRISTIANO: Camilla's daughter!

CLARITA: Camilla's son!

CRISTIANO: White woman's daughter!

CLARITA: White woman's son!

(Clarita, four years old, and his cousin Cristiano, twelve, performing a wordfight)

Anthropologists of childhood have long examined the complex and diverse strategies that children employ to gain and affirm power in the peer group, arguing that language and children's creative use of words is often central to this. However, most of this research has taken place in industrialized contexts across Europe and North America, and much less has been written on peer group dynamics and children's creative use of language in hunter-gatherer societies. Yet the peer group is a crucial space of learning for hunter-gatherer children, who spend most of their time playing together and away from adult supervision, teaching each other how to act and behave properly. A closer look to peer group relations is therefore essential to understand child socialization in a hunter-gatherer context.[1]

Starting with an analysis of *wordfights*—verbal confrontations that take the form of a ritualized exchange of insults, like the one above between Clarita and Cristiano—this chapter explores the strategies through which Matses children teach each other appropriate skills and attitudes they will need to become competent, grown-up social actors. My primary focus is on Matses boys and how they use language as a tool to push each other to grow into *dadambo* men, reproducing values and ideas of masculinity that are well established among previous generations. At the same time, new imageries of masculinity originating in the outside world and globalized media are challenging these views and offering new materials that children can use to craft a new sense of who they are and what kind of men they want to be in the future. And by developing aspirations and desires for new forms of masculinity, the children actively reinvent the meanings of boyhood, leading to radical change.[2]

Wordfights and the Physical Power of Speech

The dialogue reported above between four-year-old Clarita and her twelve-year-old cousin Cristiano is an instance of a wordfight, an act that is regularly performed by Matses children but has no specific term in Matses language (to my knowledge, this type of verbal interaction has not been documented for any other society or group in Amazonia). Wordfights generally start with two children having a disagreement and getting angry at each other, at which point one insults the other, and they start exchanging insults. The insults are not random but take a standardized, epithetical structure that likens the opponent child to something hideous. For example, Clarita and Cristiano call each other "bat ears" (as in "You have ears like a bat"), "dolphin nose," and "spider legs" but also "white woman's daughter," "white woman's son," and so forth.

The key to winning a wordfight is to be creative and able to think fast of new insults to shout at the opposing child. The child who cannot make up insults quickly and is left speechless loses the fight, or as the children say, *perdeuaic*, a term they have adapted from the Spanish "to lose," whereas the child who shouts the last insult *ganauiac*, "wins." Wordfighting is not experienced as play or cheerful banter but as a verbal duel arising from real anger, and the children describe losing a wordfight as dreadful and humiliating. Wordfights often take place in front of an audience of other children, who can step in and suggest insults to the fighters when they run short, ensuring the fight continues, and the combatants themselves can be seen looking around for new ideas for insults. For example, as they saw me approaching, Clarita and Cristiano found new inspiration and called each other "white woman's daughter" and "white woman's son."

The power of insults lies not in the semantic or literal meaning of an utterance as much as in the performative nature of the duel, where any formulaic epithet assumes an offensive connotation. A child is not hurt by the insult itself, that is, being called "white woman's son" or "bat ears," but rather humiliated and put down when unable to find any comeback. As such, the meaning of these wordfights can be understood through what J. L. Austin termed "illocutionary force" (1962: 105), denoting a kind of power contained in certain utterances that are not so much aimed at conveying semantic meaning or at describing things but rather at influencing behavior. As the children explain, the point of a wordfight is to reduce one's opponent to being *natiec*, a term that can be translated as "paralyzed with embarrassment" and "unable to do a thing." The Matses describe being *natiec* as a full-body and emotional state marked by a mixture of embarrassment, hurt, fear, and shyness in front of others. As the children phrased it, "When you're *natiec*, you can't move! You feel ashamed and you feel like crying, but everyone is watching you, so you try not to cry. Your face becomes all red and your chest feels hot, your neck gets all stiff, and you feel like you can't move. That is what being *natiec* means."

The children are well aware of the illocutionary force of speech (i.e., its capacity to influence physical behavior) and use it accordingly in wordfights to try and reduce the opponent child to this *natiec*, paralyzed-with-embarrassment state. The worst possible reaction a child can have when attacked by another is to burst into tears, which will prompt everyone else to laugh and call the crying child a *lluvi-lluvi*, or "crybaby"—even grown adults still recall the feeling of being *natiec* when they lost a wordfight with another child as a dreadful experience.

A child's capacity to restrain another's behavior through the illocutionary force of spoken words is a crucial tool in Matses peer groups, where anger is managed *exclusively* through words and physical violence is entirely absent. This was one of the most astonishing findings from my fieldwork: in the many months I have spent with Matses children over the past decade, not once have I witnessed a child (or an adult) engaging in a physical fight, with the very rare exception of little children below the age of three fighting with their siblings. Boys wrestle for fun, and children might push and punch each other on the arm in a confrontational manner, but they never hit others to intentionally cause physical harm or take out their anger at one another.

This might seem surprising, even contradictory in a culture that praises tough masculinity and has a long tradition of warfare, where until recently not just grown men but also children would take part in raiding expeditions. But Matses people are extremely critical of public displays of anger, and physical aggression is inadmissible, as in other Indigenous groups across Amazonia. Joanna Overing and Alan Passes highlighted this apparent contradiction in their famous collection of works on love and anger in Amazonia (2000), where a number of ethnographers showed that adults actively discourage children from

displaying anger in an uncontrolled manner, teaching them instead to chan-
nel their rage through ritualized acts (see also Mezzenzana 2020).

Likewise, when Matses children feel *nëisha* (angry), they take their rage out
through words and use verbal aggression to control and attack each other. These
verbal confrontations are at the very core of Matses children's peer group interactions, and thus a mastery of words is a vital skill for dealing with others and
negotiating tensions and conflicts. The wordfight is only one type of interaction,
but it emphasizes the importance of aggressive speech, as well as the creative
use of the spoken word as essential tools within peer-group dynamics. In the following sections I will focus on other, more flexible forms of language and
aggressive verbal exchanges through which children learn to affirm their roles
and power in relation to others.

Crafting Guns and Becoming *Dadambo*: The Ethical Value of Verbal Confrontations

"Where's your mother, Paco?" asks Nelson. He puts his gun down and fixes
Paco with a steady gaze. Paco shuts up, his gun still in his hands. He lowers his head and frowns. All the boys around them become quiet and
stop crafting their guns, watching Paco's face intently. They want to see
if he'll cry.

Nelson says nothing else. He takes his gun and keeps working at it.
For a while beforehand, Paco had been making fun of Nelson's gun, calling it badly made and ugly, while the other boys sat down quietly working on their own guns. Nelson had kept quiet for a bit, struggling to craft
his gun, until he got fed up with Paco's mockery. That's when he looked
at Paco, calmly, and asked, "Where's your mother?"

We all know where Paco's mother is. She lives in a different village,
with her new husband. When Paco's father left for the city, she ran
away with another man, leaving Paco with his grandparents in the village. Paco's mother *niana* ("abandoned him," as the children say).

Nelson's question has brought silence to the group and caused Paco
to be *natiec*, "unable to do anything," with embarrassment and discomfort. His eyes are shiny, his forehead wrinkled. He looks about to burst
into tears. Paco's gun is good, but he has no weapon against Nelson—in
a verbal confrontation, the boy who stays speechless is defeated. Paco
has lost.

I have witnessed the whole scene, watching the boys crafting guns
with tree bark and small knives (see figure 23). They know me well now
and let me hang out with them, unlike any other adult, and I am grateful
to have earned this privilege. I wonder if I should intervene and tell

FIGURE 23 Crafting guns and playing war (photographs by John, ten years old).

Nelson off. But his words have disarmed me too: I feel sorry for Paco, abandoned by his mother, and I am shocked at the ease with which his peer mocks him for it. Meanwhile, Nelson sits in front of us, looking unmoved.

Once the guns are finished, the war begins. The boys split up into two opposing army-teams. All the boys scream, "Nelson! I want to be with Nelson!" Nelson smirks and chooses his teammates. A couple of boys who are left in the rival team, with Paco, complain and protest in disappointment. "We are the Estados Unidos," the United States, shouts Nelson. He then calls the other team *Japon*, Japan, the losing team.

This episode highlights a crucial quality every Matses child should develop: that of being *cuididi*, a term that can be translated as a "mischievous boy" or a "naughty troublemaker." The term applies primarily to boys, where the equivalent for girls is *chishpida* (naughty girl), but *cuididi* can be used for both genders in the plural form, for example when Matses adults yell at children *cuididiquenda*, "Stop acting naughty!" A *cuididi* child is one who pushes the rules of acceptable behavior, who knows how to respond to other children's teasing and insults, and who shows to be fearless of other children's attacks and the scolding of adults. The Matses say that being naughty is *bacuebön padibi* (children's nature), much as being *dadambo* is the nature of men and being *dayac* that of women, and just like these qualities, the ability to be *cuididi* must be developed and affirmed through repeated action.

In the children's peer group, this is done on a daily basis through verbal confrontations. A *cuididi* boy knows how to verbally attack, mock, and insult others and is adept at counterattacking without showing any signs of weakness. Nelson offers an example of this. He will not stand for mockery and uses his power to stop Paco by asking, "Where's your mother?," knowing this question will leave him speechless. By having the last word he affirms himself as *cuididi*, gaining the respect of all the other children, who side with him and shout "I want to play with Nelson!"

Nelson, eleven years old, is the oldest boy in the group and the most *cuididi*. Paco is one year younger, shyer and not as loud as Nelson. More importantly, Paco has a weak spot that the other children can use to defeat him in any kind of verbal quarrel: his mother, as he lives with his aunt and is the only child in the entire village who has been abandoned by both parents. The children are well aware of the illocutionary force contained in the word "mother" for Paco, and Nelson asks his question rhetorically with the intention to influence behavior and make him *natiec*. "Mother" thus becomes a "lived word" that is "freely communicated and understood at the social level" but that people also inhabit "in the form of specific biographical associations, emotional attachments and bodily states that can be substantially, even radically, discrepant from those of another person" (Irving 2011: 346).

While this interaction might appear to display a fundamental lack of empathy, or even as an act of bullying, it is the very opposite. The children's attitude must be understood in relation to Matses ethics, where being tough and fierce is not only desirable but necessary to survive in the world, as can be better explained through another episode that took place during my first year of fieldwork, when I was drawing with the children in school. Enrique, the schoolteacher, would occasionally ask me to replace him in school and teach English to the children or carry out creative activities using the abundant stationery materials I had brought with me: felt-tip pens, colored pencils, rubbers, paper sheets, notebooks, and crêpe paper, which I gave out generously and used as part of creative research methodologies, alongside the digital cameras and sound-recorder used for filming and photographic projects with the children. This is very unusual, since schoolteachers generally only distribute a few notebooks and very small amounts of stationery, so the children very much enjoyed being in school when I was replacing their teacher. But at the same time, the children saw me as a playing companion rather than an authoritative adult, and whenever I was there, the classroom would turn into a playing field, as on the occasion described in the following excerpt from my fieldnotes.

The children and I have been modeling mud in school, and now that we'veve finished, the classroom is covered in mud and paint, and I ask the children to help me clean up. The children love cleaning, like any other activity that requires dynamism and hard work, but they also take it as an opportunity to get rowdy. They start throwing water on the desks and at each other, running around, shouting and laughing. The classroom turns wild: water and paint flow all over and children jump and run everywhere, while the heat seems to get stronger and the room louder than ever, echoing with the children's laughs and screams. In the midst of the chaos, which I fail to control, I notice two boys, Tim and Juan, arguing over a broom. I pay little attention to them, being overwhelmed by the confusion. But as I leave the classroom to throw dust outside and walk back in, I find Tim in tears. Juan holds the broom, smiling and bouncing around.

Tim is six years old and very small. He has just started school, and he seems much shyer and quieter than older boys. Juan is nine years old and he is only temporarily spending time in the village, where his parents have come to spend some time with his grandfather. Juan is a real *cuididi*: he is incredibly energetic, rarely listens to adults' commands, never sits still in school and always has a mischievous smile on his face. The other boys seem to enjoy his presence very much and always seek out his company, wanting to play with him.

As I see Tim crying, I try to gain control and comfort him, asking what's happened, but Tim just keeps sobbing. I feel moved by the sight of such a small boy in distress, with his face covered in tears. I turn to Juan and ask him whether he has hit Tim to steal his broom, as I suspect. Juan looks at me with his usual naughty grin and replies he has done nothing.

At this point Emanuel, ten years old, steps in to take Juan's side. He yells at me: "Camilla, it's not Juan's fault! He didn't hit Tim; he got the broom first." As he says this, he comes toward Tim, punches him on the shoulder and yells at him, "Stop crying, Tim!" A few other boys come over and tell me that Juan has done nothing wrong. I ask the boys why, in this case, Tim is crying so much, and they reply that he is a baby who always cries *abembi*, "for no reason" or "just for the sake of it." One by one they walk by and punch Tim's shoulder, yelling at him to stop acting like a crybaby, and then they walk away. Tim cries even more as I watch the scene, astonished.

This episode reveals some crucial values in Matses society about children and education and how these contrast with traditional Western attitudes. In the words of David Lancy (2008), children in most industrialized societies are understood as "vulnerable cherubs" who need to be protected and safeguarded, as demonstrated in my attitude to Tim both when I try to comfort him and when I react with shock at the children's seeming lack of compassion. But for Matses people, children and adults alike, my attitude is not just questionable; it is damaging and unethical. Comforting a child who cries *abembi* will make the child spoiled, and no matter how upset they are, children must be discouraged from crying unless they have a valid reason to. A child who cries *abembi* should be yelled at louder, not comforted, so she or he can toughen up and act like a *cuididi* instead of a crybaby.

Indeed, people in the village occasionally pointed out that I am too soft with children, who should be treated harshly when they misbehave or act spoiled. Another day, the primary school children whom I would usually teach had been drawing using watercolors. They left the classroom for a short break, leaving the drawings on their desks and waiting for the color to dry. While they were outside, the smaller children from the kindergarten class, aged around three to five years old, who were also on a school break, walked into the classroom and started touching the drawings and playing with them. I told them to stop and leave the drawings alone, but they did not pay much attention to me. When the primary school children walked back into the classroom, they started screaming and shooing away the smaller ones, angrily. Harry, an eight-year-old boy, saw that I was in the classroom and began to yell at me: "Look, Camilla, these babies are playing with our drawings, and what do you do?! Nothing! Why aren't you yelling at them?!"

Harry's passionate outburst reveals our contrasting attitudes—that is, my own vis-à-vis that of Matses people—toward disciplining younger and misbehaving children, which in Matses society is not only the task of adults but that of older children too. Because they spend most of their time playing together, away from adult supervision, Matses children discipline each other, and this includes discouraging socially undesirable behavior, especially in younger children like Tim, who are less socialized and thus have yet to learn how to behave "properly." What Tim did in the classroom is considered extremely inappropriate for children and especially for boys, who should learn to be strong and able to reply to verbal attacks and confrontations without bursting into tears. As such, the other boys saw their role as being to teach him how to behave in a more grown-up manner. As part of this, older children often target younger ones who cry for no reason, and play what I will term the *uaca* game, of which the following vignette shows an example.

> A group of boys and girls are gathered together laughing and joking. One
> of them is John, a *cuididi* ten-year-old. Tim approaches the group. As they
> see him coming over, John and Nelson start shouting: "Look, Tim is com-
> ing! Say *ua*, Tim! *Ua, ua, ua!*" Tim sulks and looks as if he is trying hard to
> resist crying. The boys point their fingers at him, and they keep going:
> "Say *ua, ua, ua.*" Tim lowers his head, hides his face, turns around and
> walks back in the direction he came from, drying tears from his eyes with
> his small hands. The children around me, both girls and boys, burst out
> laughing. I shout, "Come on, Tim, come back! They're only joking!" but
> he walks away. The children keep laughing.

Uaca is an onomatopoeic made-up word that means "Say *ua*," where *ua* is the sound of crying (*ua, ua, ua*). The older children play this game for fun with younger ones who cry easily, targeting both boys and girls and trying to make them *natiec* on purpose. Young adults told me they too had played and been tar-geted in the *uaca* game when they were young children, and described it as a dreadful experience that led to discomfort and isolation by their peers if they cried. Tim is still young, but he must learn to be strong if he wants to survive in the peer group and not be scorned by the older boys.

By contrast, a boy who does *not* cry, even when he has a good reason, will be much praised—as was Francisco (the nine-year-old boy I showed in chapter 1, holding a large catfish) after he smashed his head onto a log while playing in the river, suffering an injury. His father took him to the *posta*, a rudimentary health clinic in the village that stores basic medical supplies and where Felipe, a Matses man trained as a paramedic, provides basic medical assistance. Felipe bandaged the injury while a small crowd of people, including myself, gathered around him. Francisco grimaced with pain as blood ran down his forehead, but while his eyes shone, he did not shed a tear. His father stood next to him with a wide, proud smile, as he and other people praised Francisco and called him *dad-ambo*, a "real man": while Francisco is not yet a man, his courage and strength are to be praised as such.

As it is clear, being tough and able to show strength without crying is linked to being *dadambo*, which, as I discussed in previous chapters, is not just desir-able but necessary to grow into an adult man. Crying for no reason is the nega-tion of this ideal, and it is exactly the kind of attitude that Matses elders despise in the *chotac*, who are soft, weak, and incapable of working hard. In this view, playing the *uaca* game and scolding a boy who cries for no reason are not exam-ples of a lack of compassion but rather deeply ethical acts that push younger children to develop strength and resilience and therefore the skills they need to become a competent Matses adult.

After about five years on from the time we were modeling mud in school, during one of my regular yearly visits to the village, I found Tim grown up and much changed. He had lost his shy and vulnerable mien and now displayed a full-on *cuididi* attitude, ordering around a crowd of smaller kids who seemed to follow him everywhere, wanting to play with him. I joked about this drastic transformation with Tim and the other children. "Tim, you used to be such a crybaby!" I said; "the older boys used to tell you *uaca* all the time!" The adults and children who heard me recount this story found it amusing and teased Tim about it. But what was even more surprising is that nobody seemed to remember it—including Tim, who also laughed upon hearing it. People told me that this is what happens with all children, so to them there was nothing surprising or memorable about Tim's transformation.

There is therefore a kind of social order that is maintained between the generations, where children push each other to become *cuididi* in a path toward becoming strong, *dadambo* men (or *dayac* women). However, the boys are also increasingly being presented with emerging forms of masculinity that break with the values of previous generations and as a result are projecting their adulthoods toward new directions.

Diego and Jean-Claude Van Damme: Breaking with Traditional Masculinity

"No me mates, amigo!" The children run around, pointing their weapons at each other and mimicking the noise of machine guns shooting as they play war. The boys laugh and push each other jokingly; the oldest kids grab the smaller ones by the arm and pull them away as captives; the young children try to escape and beg for forgiveness in Spanish, shouting phrases in Spanish like the above, "Don't kill me, my friend!," which they learned from dubbed Jean-Claude Van Damme movies.

Nelson leads the winning team and, as he seems to always do, he has again called his team the Estados Unidos. I run around with the children, who proudly show me their captives and invite me to follow them into their secret war shelters: small havens in the greenery areas around and behind the houses, where the adults never spend time but the children occasionally play. Nelson holds the greatest number of captives, unsurprisingly.

All of a sudden one of the boys screams, *"Diego is coming!"* Nelson freezes. He stops shouting and running around. He giggles and hesitates, blushing and looking embarrassed. He watches Diego coming over and hesitates over his next move, looking awkward and embarrassed. The boys around him are still playing, but Nelson has lost his fierce warrior manner, and seemingly his interest in the game.

I turn around and see him. Diego is coming toward us, walking firmly and holding his head high, with his shoulders pushed back and his eyes fixed on us. "Don't you play this game, Diego?" I ask. "No," he replies, watching the scene with a confident and mock smile. "Why not?" I ask again. "Because it's a game for babies." As soon as he hears that, Nelson drops his gun and screams, "I'm off with Diego!" The other boys look puzzled. Nelson puts his arm over Diego's shoulder, laughing. The two boys walk away together, looking for another place to cause trouble.

Diego is thirteen years old, which means that he is too young to spend time with the adults and play football with them at dusk, but he has started spending less time in the children's peer group. He spends much time with his sixteen-year-old brother Mateo (with whom he opened the small store in the village), and he still hangs out with younger boys, especially Nelson, but he would not take part in their pretend games. Children and adults address him as the most mischievous boy in the village or *cuididimbo*, the superlative form meaning "really naughty." He is tough and verbally aggressive, and appears unafraid of receiving a scolding from the adults. His confidence shows in bodily posture and movements: Diego usually walks slowly, with his head high, shoulders pushed back, and looking people straight in the eyes. He displays a swaggering confidence when interacting with other children, is full of attitude and at times can be extremely confrontational. When he is around, the other boys always seem cautious.

In the episode above, Diego's arrival elicits a dramatic change in Nelson and impacts his entire bodily demeanor. Nelson gets embarrassed in front of Diego, who is tougher than he is. He starts giggling and moving in a clumsy way, and he blushes and looks away. And by mocking the war game Diego reaffirms himself as the toughest boy in the village and turns Nelson from a *cuididi* into a *bacuëmpi* (baby), offering another example of how the illocutionary power of speech can be used to transform behavior. One of the crucial points argued by scholars who have examined the peer group as a central site of child socialization is that peer group identities—such as that of troublemaker vis-à-vis babyish child—are "achieved rather than ascribed" (Goodwin 2006: 3), meaning that they must be continuously reaffirmed through repeated action.

Likewise, in a Matses peer group, being a tough troublemaker is not a fixed quality but rather a relational skill, an ability that emerges through confrontations with others that must be periodically restated by proving one's mischievousness not just with peers but also with the adults. One evening, when it was already dark, a few boys had come to look for me and stood outside my window. They were laughing and talking loudly, and hearing the noise, an elderly woman known as Felipa-*macho*, "Old Felipa," yelled at them: "Leave Camilla alone, or I will come over there and give you frog poison!" Old Felipa grew up before contact, and the children are scared of her because she is fierce and often forces small children to take frog poison if they are misbehaving. The children have given her the Spanish nickname *policía*, "policewoman," a word they learned in town and by watching television. As they heard her yell, the boys shut up, terrified, knowing that Old Felipa would follow up on her threat. But not Diego, who instead of quietening down yelled back at her: "Leave us alone, Old Felipa! Go to sleep with your old husband!" The boys exploded with laughter. Old Felipa did not reply, most likely because she did not hear Diego, but for weeks the children kept recounting this episode, praising Diego for his fearless and mischievous gesture. Affirming one's identity as *cuididi* is a delicate and continuous process of pushing the boundary of accepted behavior in this way while avoiding punishment.

When I got to know Diego better, he started extending his mischievous behavior to our interactions: he insulted me, mocked me for my habit of asking numerous and repetitive questions, and would speak to me more like a playing companion than an adult, as the other children also did. At the same time, he was extremely curious about my research and always volunteered to help, whether through drawing, taking photographs, or chatting about various topics, and I gained some of my most important insights into children's ways of knowing through my interactions with him. Like the other children, Diego was fascinated by my presence and often asked me questions about my homeland, my friends and what we do together, whether I had ever seen or been inside a car, and how much money my camera and laptop cost, revealing an enchantment with the *chotac* world I represented. He was one of the leaders among the boys at the beginning of my fieldwork, when I could not yet speak Matses, asking me to take pictures of them as they reenacted scenes from Jean-Claude Van Damme movies.

Van Damme was one of Diego's favorite topics of conversation. He would often ask me to take photographs of him with his T-shirt wrapped around his head, posing like a character from Hollywood action movies (figure 24). The same is true of the other children, who are only occasionally able to watch movies yet whose talk, drawings, and play are filled with them on a daily basis. The games described above are an example of this: their crafting of guns and war games are derived from the imagery of Hollywood movies, as further suggested by the children identifying the winning team as the United States and the losing one as Japan. (When I asked them what Japan is, the children told me that "Japan is an army of soldiers who live in a tunnel under the ground," and I eventually understood they were referring to a Hollywood movie on the Vietnam-American war and calling Vietnamese soldiers *Japón*). Likewise, many of the photographs I collected during fieldwork, when I began to distribute digital cameras to the children, showed them reproducing fighting scenes in Jean-Claude Van Damme's

FIGURE 24 Diego dressed up like a ninja character (photograph by Paco, ten years old).

style, revealing how children make globalized imageries part of their everyday worlds (figure 25).

Various scholars have documented young men's fascination with action movies in rural and Indigenous societies with established traditions of warfare and hunting (High 2010; Kulick and Willson 1994; Wood 2006). In these contexts, figures like Rambo and Bruce Lee are understood as presenting young men with new images of male power that fit into localized, traditional understandings of masculinity. Michael Wood argues that for young Kamula men in Papua New Guinea, "Rambo came to stand for forms of masculine and sovereign power that he could transfer into the social body of Kamula men," as a figure that young men "could identify with and thereby explore new understandings of masculinity" (2006: 62). Likewise, Casey High shows that young Waorani men in Amazonian Ecuador praise their ancestors as skilled hunters and spear-fighters,

FIGURE 25 Children perform Jean-Claude Van Damme moves (photographs by Harry, eight years old, and Paco, ten).

although physical violence and warfare are no longer acceptable for them—and in this context, "images of Bruce Lee and Rambo appear to embody a fantasy of masculine power and generational continuity that young men idealize, even if they fail to demonstrate it in everyday life" (2010: 762).

Jean-Claude Van Damme can also be seen as embodying traditional values of masculinity that are being passed down through the generations and which boys look up to in their path toward becoming *dadambo*. He is strong, agile, dynamic, brave and a fearless *cuesnanquid*, a "fighter," much like the boys' grandfathers were when they were young and raided neighboring groups. Van Damme's popularity among the boys indicates a degree of continuity in the values and ideals of being a man. But there is also a fundamental rupture occurring, as rendered graphically in a drawing by Nelson (figure 26), where he portrays

FIGURE 26 Matses warriors fight Jean-Claude Van Damme (drawing by Nelson, eleven years old).

a group of Matses warriors (on the left) fighting against Jean-Claude Van Damme and his army (on the right).

This imaginary war scene conflates the oral histories of warfare told by Nelson's grandfathers with new images of masculinity brought in by globalized media, specifically movies, both of which equate masculinity to warriorhood. But while the Matses elders fight with bows and arrows and a single old shotgun, Jean-Claude Van Damme and his army counterattack with a helicopter, an army tank, and machine guns that spit red and yellow flames. I asked Nelson who wins this war, and without hesitation, he replied, "*Vandán!*"

While embodying traditional masculine values of strength and bravery, these new images of warriorhood also depart from the traditional masculinity of Matses elders and shift toward new possible ways of being a man. Tony Simpson argues in relation his work with young men in Zambia that "global forces necessarily play an important role in the construction of masculine identities and the local can only be understood within larger global frames" (2009: 5), and here Matses boys are presented with new imageries of masculinity to be looked up to while also feeling out of reach. When I asked them to describe him to me and to explain why they like him so much, girls and boys alike told me that "*Vandán* is very tall," as opposed to Matses people, who are shorter; "he is *chotac* and white," while Matses boys define themselves as *chëshë* (black); and finally, "he has lot of money and numerous girlfriends," all signs of great prestige for

Matses children. As Nelson's certainty about the outcome of his imagined battle suggests, this is a *winning* type of masculinity: one that is in many ways preferable to the ways of being of their elders.

Similarly to how the girls play with dolls and learn to value the skills and looks of *chotac* women, so Matses boys are placing value on new masculinities that originate in the outside world and lead to gender subversion. For example, Diego is entering puberty and on the verge of becoming a man. Throughout his childhood, he has mastered the quintessentially masculine skills of showing courage, being able to handle other children's attacks and attacking back, establishing his own *cuididi* identity in relation to others, and placing himself on the right path to becoming a real man, like his own father. However, his ideal of masculinity is now defined by new values and qualities, such as the ability to make money, travel to and spend time in the city, and learn how to act like a *chotac* man, which are driving him away from the kind of man his father is. These new desires—and their tangible consequences—can only be fully understood by exploring children's fascination with the *chotac* urban world, which is the subject of the next chapter.

6

Yearning for Concrete

Children's Imagination as a Catalyst for Change

I opened the book with a drawing by Paloma, the six-year-old girl who drew herself and her mother traveling in a car in the city, Iquitos, where she has never been. Her drawing was among many others where children portrayed *chotac* places, people, and objects, many of which they had no direct experience of. Here I want to look closely at drawing as a method of research and representation and a situated activity that allows children to transcend their immediate surroundings and access a distant elsewhere that remains physically unreachable, blurring the boundaries between the real and the imagined. Matses children's drawings open a window onto their frequent imaginary journeys to the *chotac yacno*, meaning "places where *chotac* people live" or "non-Indigenous territory," suggesting how they engage, even though at a distance, with the materiality of urban landscapes and alternative ways of living.

Imagining as Being-There

The drawing by eight-year-old Billy (figure 27) shows a *chotac* man walking through Colonia Angamos. Originally founded in the 1980s as a military garrison, Colonia Angamos later expanded into a small rural town and became the seat of the Yaquerana district, which is part of the Loreto department of Peru, under whose jurisdiction Matses villages fall. The town now has a rural clinic, a local municipality, an airstrip, a school, and several *bodegas*, small stores selling clothes, kitchen goods, flashlights, batteries, petrol, and packaged food such as biscuits, rice, and cooking oil. Most Matses families travel to town two or three times a year to purchase goods and visit the clinic, and in recent years many have also built cheap and low-maintenance houses made of forest materials at the outskirts of it (while the concrete houses of the *chotac* are located at the center). Those who visit can only afford to spend limited periods of time in town,

FIGURE 27 A *chotac* man walks through town (drawing by Billy, nine years old).

however, as living there requires money to buy food and, as Matses people often lament, *piucquid nidbëdec*: they have "no money."

Matses children and teenagers complain that they would like to spend much more time in town, where they can walk on concrete, watch television, and eat packaged food. While this is an isolated rural settlement, Matses people, especially the children, refer to it as a place of great opportunity compared with their local villages, as emphasized in Billy's drawing. The purple base at the bottom is a concrete pavement, while the tall purple shape in the top right is a water cistern, showing that the town, unlike his forest village, has clear running water. The big green structure on the left-hand side is a lamppost, and the circles attached to the houses are houselights: it is nighttime in the drawing, and as Billy explained, the *chotac* man can walk around the town fully illuminated by artificial light, and people can have a social nightlife there (although public electricity is only available for about two hours after sunset, given the limited funds of the local municipality). Billy also pointed out that the *chotac* man wears shoes and long trousers, which are very expensive items much desired by Matses children but can only be obtained using money, suggesting that *chotac* people are permitted different possibilities of action also because, as Billy himself told me, *aton piucquid dadpen icquec*: this man "has plenty of money" and can afford things that are not available to most Matses people, such as nice clothes and shoes.

Drawing is a useful ethnographic method, distinct from film or photography, which can be used to access people's imaginations, understandings, and creativity while simultaneously being a mode of representation. Researchers of childhood recognize it as an invaluable technique that can help explore children's cognitive understandings at levels beyond those for which they have words (Mead 1932; Toren 1999, 2007) while granting them a great deal of freedom in terms of how and what they choose to represent (White et al. 2010; Young and Barrett 2001). But they also stress that, when looking at children's drawings, it is essential to consider "not only the content of an image, but also the circumstances of its production" (Mitchell 2006: 63), and here it is worth noting that while the drawings were produced in various situations (individually and collectively, in school and outside of school, at the children's own spontaneous request or following my elicitation), in most cases the children themselves initiated the drawing activity, and in most instances they chose to portray objects, people, and elements associated with the *chotac yacno*.

As such, drawing opens up a window onto the imaginary journeys through which children move beyond the horizons of their everyday villages and access what Vincent Crapanzano describes as the "hinterland," that is, "a very concrete land, a place, an intimate one, . . . which lies elsewhere, *ailleurs*, beyond where one is and yet intimately related to it" (2004: 15). The imagination, and drawing as a tangible expression of it, is more than a portrayal of "inner" imaginaries or ideas: it is also a way of bringing to life the *chotac* world and engaging with it, as can be appreciated by framing the analysis of these drawings within a Heideggerian theory of knowledge and expression. For Heidegger, knowing is not just a process through which notions are "stored up in the cabinet of consciousness" (1962 [1927]: 89) but rather a dynamic way of *being-there* with the entities that are known. In his words, "If I 'merely' know about some ways in which the being of entities is interconnected, if I 'only' represent them, if I do no more than 'think' about them, I am no less alongside the entities outside in the world that when I *originally* grasp them" (89–90; emphasis in original).

Knowing (and expressing what is known) is here understood as a way of being-there with the entities that are known and of engaging with them through certain emotional feelings, a specific mood, or what Heidegger calls a "state of mind" (172). By extending this view to the imagination as itself a form of knowledge and to drawing as a mode of expressing this knowledge, I propose that by imagining and drawing the *chotac* world, the children are actively engaging with it, even if at a distance, and establishing a relationship with this part of the world founded on feelings of fascination, desire, and *yearning*. As such, imagining the *chotac* world is a way of being-there with concrete, electric light, *chotac* people, and other desirable but faraway entities, and in the very act of imagining these entities, the children become affectively attached to them—as suggested by Paloma when she says, "I love concrete."

Drawing is an expression of this yearning. In Michael Taussig's words, drawing is not only a "means of witness" but also "a hauling, an unravelling, and *being impelled towards* something or somebody" (2011: xii; emphasis added) and is hence itself a form of movement. Matses children's representations of the *chotac yacno* indeed suggest their *being impelled toward* this distant world that remains out of physical reach, while at the same time revealing a perceived *impossibility* of moving and a growing sense of marginalization and exclusion.

The Implications of Children's Imaginings

The imagination offers a way for people to move beyond the horizon of their everyday surroundings, but at the same time, imagining always takes place in an environment, and children's feelings of fascination and desire for a distant elsewhere always unfold within the recognition of a tangible here-and-now. Matses children's imagination of the *chotac yacno* as an alluring place only makes sense as it emerges in opposition to their everyday dwellings, and their drawings display a dichotomy between urban and rural life that highlights the restrictions encountered in their everyday villages, as exemplified in the contrasting images drawn by two Matses girls (figure 28).

The drawing by nine-year-old Romina represents Colonia Angamos (figure 28, top). All the houses look identical because, as Romina explained, they are all made of concrete and *cemento bëdamboshë icquec*, "concrete is great." In Matses language, the Spanish term *cemento* refers to concrete, cement, tarmac, and also to the concrete pavements that connect the various houses in Colonia Angamos, cutting across the grassy and earthy ground of the town, as shown in Romina's drawing. The disruption of perspectives here is partly due to Romina's ability as a nine-year-old girl to draw and to coordinate visual stimuli, memory inputs, the nervous system, and the hand doing the drawing, but this irregular assemblage of structures can also be said to reveal something of how she imagines and perceives the place from a great distance. The enormous paths in the middle of the drawing emphasize the centrality of concrete to life in the town and reinforce that when children imagine the *chotac yacno* at a distance, they perceive concrete as a dominant material, as suggested by the following dialogue between Paloma and myself:

PALOMA: Is there concrete in your land, Camilla?

CAMILLA: Yes, there is plenty of it.

PALOMA: I see.

CAMILLA: Do you like concrete, Paloma?

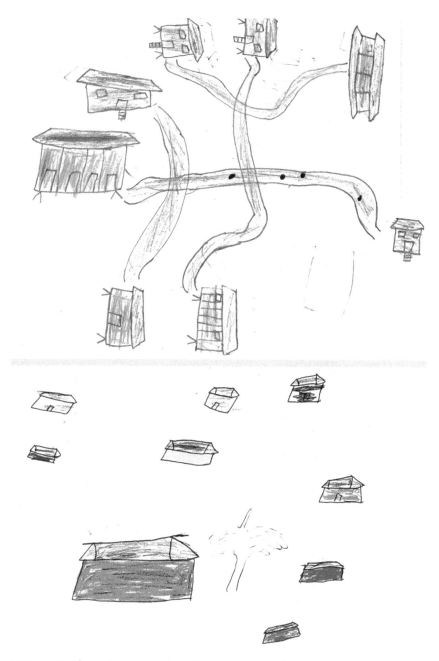

FIGURE 28 *Above*: the town of Colonia Angamos (drawing by Romina, nine years old). *Below*: the village (drawing by Lily, nine years old).

PALOMA: Yes! I love concrete!

CAMILLA: Why do you like it?

PALOMA: It's good. Good for walking. Good for running.

CAMILLA: Is soil not good for walking?

PALOMA: No. It's painful. Concrete is great. I love concrete [literally, "I crave concrete"].

In Paloma's drawing of Iquitos at the beginning of this book, some of the most prominent features are giant black houses and *cemento* streets, for as Paloma confidently explained to me, in Iquitos even people's houses are made of concrete, and the farther away one moves from Matses territory, the more concrete can be found. I once asked seven-year-old Matias how he imagines my homeland, and his face brightened up as he replied, with no hesitation, "*cemento-ic-pambo*" (All made of concrete). The concrete world stands in contrast to the village where the children live, represented in the second drawing, by nine-year-old Lily (figure 28, bottom). Matses houses are smaller and more colorful than those in the town, for as Lily explained, they are built using forest materials. A big tree stands in the middle of the drawing, giving a sense of the thick, bright green vegetation that surrounds the houses.

In the village there is only one small concrete pavement, badly constructed and weather-beaten, which was built a few years ago by the regional municipality of Colonia Angamos, likely in an attempt to gain popularity with the large Matses voting bloc. Because of the significance of the Matses population within the local electorate, candidates running for mayor invest in long and loud campaigns of propaganda to gain their votes, organize community events, buy food and gasoline for Matses communities, or even buy goods for individuals who promise to vote for them. Elected mayors who run for a second term engage in even bigger gestures using public funds, such as renovating the school buildings in the community or building concrete pavements like this one.

When I complained to them about how useless I found the path, young people and especially children replied they are very fond of it and would like even more concrete in their communities. They often walk barefoot on the ground, which is full of thorns and spiky plants that hurt their feet, and during the rainy season some parts of the village become so muddy that it is impossible to walk around and get to the end of the day with clean feet. Harry, an eight-year-old boy, told me that walking barefoot is unpleasant because the soil is *mata-mata-pambo*, "all muddy" or literally "painfully muddy," while concrete makes walking much easier.

The same goes for what Matses people call *luz*, the Spanish word for "light," which in Matses language has come to signify electric light, as well as houselights, electricity, and the infrastructure of power lines and lampposts found in town.

Children say that *luz bëdamboshë icquec* (electric light is great) and complain about the lack of electricity in their village. For them, electricity and artificial light are a special *"affordance"* of town, a term that Tim Ingold (1987: 2; 1992) has used to understand the material possibilities that a certain type of environment offers its living inhabitants, including animals, in relation to the type of body they have. By extending the term to the *urban* environment, both concrete and electric light can be understood as resources that afford a set of different possibilities of dwelling, moving, and interacting with others; in this case, the possibility of having a different kind of social nightlife. The adults go to bed when it gets dark, and this is the time when children from about seven years old onward enjoy going out and meeting each other, walking together, playing, chatting, and laughing. But the nights in the rainforest are so dark that not much can be done, and flashlights and batteries are among the most valuable goods for Matses children.

The drawing by ten-year-old Emanuel (figure 29, top) portrays an unspecified *chotac yacno* where three houses are connected by power lines providing electric illumination, and round shapes attached to the roofs inside the houses represent internal lights. The power lines are also linked to lampposts outside the houses, three on the left-hand side and three on the right. Emanuel pointed out that at night, the *chotac yacno* is illuminated inside and out, and people can watch television. The other drawing (figure 29, bottom), by eight-year-old Harry, shows a group of children sitting in front of a television screen in town and watching a film, something they can only do on their sporadic visits to Colonia Angamos, where the townspeople have televisions in their shops or on open patios, and Matses children often gather around and watch with them, as shown in the drawing.

When talking about and drawing electricity, concrete, and television, the children always refer to the lack of these in their own villages, and as such imagining the *chotac yacno* at a distance reaffirms children's perceived sense of inequality and the *im*possibilities of moving around and being in the forest compared with the desirable *chotac* world. "What makes the inaccessibility of the hinterland terrifying is less its inaccessibility than its determining role in our perception of that which we take naively to be accessible: that which we actually perceive, experience, touch and feel. . . . [F]or that which we perceive is always determined . . . by that absence, that imagined presence" (Crapanzano 2004: 17).

Here the imagined presence of concrete and other urban affordances is defining how children perceive the world and their place and opportunities within it. To an extent, Matses children's fascination with and desire for this part of the world reinforce "a long-standing Indigenous openness to the Other—particularly the white and mestizo Others" (Santos Granero 2009: 477), which has been widely documented in ethnographies of the region (Chaumeil 2009;

FIGURE 29 *Above*: *chotac yacno* with artificial illumination (drawing by Emanuel, ten years old). *Below*: children watch television in town (drawing by Harry, eight years old).

Ewart 2007). However, this openness must be understood in relation to recent processes of socioeconomic transformation in Matses society, which are resulting in children having radically different inclinations toward the *chotac* world compared with elderly people. As I have shown throughout the book, elderly people do not share the children's passion for the *chotac* people and lifestyles. They mention the city infrequently in their everyday speech and associate it with a range of unpleasant feelings such as boredom, loneliness, hunger, and annoyance. Most have been to the city, Iquitos, only once or twice, and although they enjoy visiting Colonia Angamos a few times a year to buy cartridges and fishing tools or to visit the local clinic, they like to keep these visits short and sporadic. For example, Julio, the man who adopted me as his sister, admits to knowing little about the *chotac yacno* yet dislikes it for many reasons. Whenever he travels to Colonia Angamos he feels lonely, for he knows no one there and misses his large family of two wives and over ten children. He has been to Iquitos only twice and recalls being overwhelmed by the noise of rickshaws and feeling hungry because he had no money and could not go hunting or fishing.

Likewise Alina, who was born shortly after missionary contact, saw Iquitos only once and remembers it being *chumboshë* (too hot) due to the concrete and tarmac all around, and that she got bored very quickly because she could not work in her cultivated field. Older Matses are not amused by walking on concrete pavements, and they complain that when young people spend time in town they *uspuec* (laze around) and sit in the house all day doing nothing. As I have mentioned, Colonia Angamos was only founded in the 1980s and did not expand into a proper town until the 1990s, meaning that until then, Matses people had limited if any experience of traveling to towns or cities at all. In a similar vein to the river environment, the children are growing up in a world where the city is already there and view it as a place full of exciting activities, whereas elderly Matses discovered it only later in life and have never developed the same feelings of fascination and desire for it.

Expectations of Non-Indigenousness
and the Trajectories of Matses Futures

One of the children's favorite activities when they visit Colonia Angamos is walking to the town's airstrip to watch airplanes taking off and landing, as shown in a drawing by the ten-year-old John (figure 30). Flights from Colonia Angamos to Iquitos are operated by the Peruvian military, and the drawing shows a soldier with a machine gun standing in front of a crowd of onlookers and passengers. Flights are supposed to run twice a week but are often canceled or postponed due to rain or other reasons. When flights are scheduled, a group of mostly children and young people walk to the airstrip and stand there to *issec* (watch

FIGURE 30 An airplane lands in Colonia Angamos (drawing by John, ten years old).

the people arriving from Iquitos and others boarding the plane). Colonia Anga-mos is the gateway to the urban world of Peruvian cities and, even farther away, that of *matses ushu* (white people like myself).

Like many of the other boys and girls, John told me that in the future he hopes to "make money" so that he can travel to Iquitos and Lima, the capital of

Peru, and perhaps even to the United States—a place made famous among the children by the Hollywood movies they watch in town. Whenever they see an international aircraft flying over their home villages, the children scream with excitement, "Plane, take me with you!" If I asked them where the airplane is traveling to, the children would usually reply, "It goes to your homeland!" and commented that *matses ushu* have plenty of money and can travel when and where they desire, whereas the Matses cannot afford to. In the children's conversation, the airplane has come to signify the symbolic and geographical divide between the land of the Matses and the outside world: while the planes can reach Matses territory, flying over their villages or landing in Colonia Angamos, Matses children cannot reach the place where the planes come from, and whenever I tried to tell young Matses that not all white people are immensely wealthy, as they imagine, they immediately replied, "Then how can you afford to fly here?," reinforcing that between them and the world of cities and of white people lies an almost unbridgeable distance. Young Matses are thus developing a sense of being marginalized within a world whose horizons have been shifting rapidly outward in recent years.

I have described mobility as a central feature of life *ënden* (in the past) when the now-elderly people were children and the Matses lived nomadically deep in the rainforest, and I showed how this mobility was not only an adaptive survival strategy but an active choice driven by people's passion for the forest. If for elderly Matses and other forest-based, hunter-gatherer Amazonians mobility meant primarily moving through the forest on foot, the young generations are expressing the desire to engage in new kinds of movement and journeys, namely, traveling to town and into *chotac* territory. But as they often remark, Matses people have no money, and the children's journeys are almost all imaginative. As such, drawing as explicitly imaginative action becomes a way to appropriate the *chotac yacno* and actively experience it on an everyday basis—in Heideggerian terms, to be-there with the town and its objects—but their drawing also displays and highlights the restrictions they encounter in the everyday world.

The children expressed this themselves when I conducted a series of filmed interviews between 2012 and 2014, asking them how they imagine their own adulthood and old age (the images in figure 31 are stills from the interviews). Although the children were interviewed individually, their answers presented striking similarities, indicating some level of agreement in their views for the future and restating many of the hopes and expectations they had so often expressed in our informal conversations and everyday dialogues.

Most of the girls told me that in the future they see themselves contributing to the household economy by fishing and working in a family field, like their mothers and grandmothers, but none mentioned accompanying their husbands to the forest on hunting treks, like the elderly women did and still do today. Instead, they all expressed the wish to marry a man who will make money and

FIGURE 31 Filmed interviews on children's imagined futures.

buy clothes for them, and some girls added that they hope to make money themselves by working as housekeepers for *chotac* families in Colonia Angamos. Most boys replied that when they grow up, they also see themselves contributing to the household by fishing and cultivating their fields, but none mentioned hunting. I asked a few of them whether they will be skilled forest dwellers in the future, to which most replied that they will not be, simply because they do not want to. Their paramount objective is to make money, so that they can travel abroad and buy packaged food and manufactured goods like machetes, knives, and flashlights in town.

The children are growing up in a world that is not confined to the forest, as it was for their grandparents, but in which the city, money, concrete, clothes, electric light, and television have become important parts of the structure of the universe, and they have to make sense of it using the resources at their disposal. The children's interviews reveal what might be termed "expectations of modernity" or, in this case, of "non-Indigenousness," which following James Ferguson I define as the desire to "gain access to the "first class things" of the world" (1999: 13). For Matses children these are new clothes, packaged food, money, journeys to the city, marrying a *chotac* partner, and so forth.

And yet the children are also developing a sense of what Ferguson terms "abjection," that is, a feeling of being "thrown aside, expelled, or discarded" and stuck in "the ranks of the 'second class'" (236) in a world where better livelihoods are attainable, but only by certain people. When I asked them *how* they plan to make money, nearly every boy I interviewed replied that in the future they will work as *madereros* (loggers), which several adult men have done in recent years, including some of their fathers, who recall it as a wearying, dreadful, and not even lucrative experience. These men had to travel far from home to a different part of the rainforest and work for *chotac* employers who took advantage of them due to their poor knowledge of Spanish and inexperience with waged jobs. Most men recount being treated badly, waking up at night to start working before sunrise, and being forced to continue until sunset without a break. Many were underpaid or, in some cases, not paid at all, and most did not save up very much.

Despite these unsuccessful experiences, of which the children are well aware, nearly all the boys in the village expressed to me the wish to work in the logging industry in the future, even though their own fathers hated it, accepting that working in the *madera*, or timber industry, is one of the very few means by which they can make money. When I asked some of the men in the village why they worked cutting timber, they replied, "*utsi nidbedeosh*" (literally, "there was nothing else to do"), reinforcing this lack of options.

Children's imagination, like playing and other childhood practices, should not be dismissed as having an end in itself but recognized as holding tangible consequences for children's concrete experiences and those of their elders. For Matses children, imagining the *chotac* world at a distance reinforces the awareness of their daily conditions and (im)possibilities: as Crapanzano put it, "the irreality of the imaginary impresses the real on reality and the real of reality compels the irreality of the imaginary" (2004: 15). Their *craving* for concrete and urban life always implies a recognition that Matses people are largely cut out of this world and have limited resources with which to access it.

The impact of children's drive toward the *chotac yacno* is becoming visible in the life choices of young Matses between the ages of eighteen and twenty-five, with a growing number choosing to leave the forest and settle in towns or cities, seeking new ways to access waged labor and enjoy urban lifestyles. In the years following the interviews reported above, I have seen a growing number of young people making this move, but owing to their low levels of education and their lack of *chotac* skills such as speaking Spanish or counting money, these attempts often fail, with young Matses becoming a new generation of slum dwellers and cheap laborers, living in poverty on the margins of Peruvian society. By longing for the world of concrete and electric light from an early age—yet already recognizing that their future attempts to appropriate this world for themselves will likely fail—Matses children are putting in place the conditions for a new type of future: one heavily based on the monetary economy and *chotac* practices but also marked by emerging forms of political marginalization and economic hardship that were not part of Matses elders' own childhood and youth. The following chapter follows the lives of these migrant youths, showing how they are evolving over time and exploring the consequences of their childhood knowledge, imaginations, and desires, not only for their own lives but for the future of Amazonia.

7

Urban Futures

When Dreams of Concrete Come True

On my last visit to the forest in 2019, I found the village looking eerily empty. During my earlier years of fieldwork, the evenings were bustling with the sounds of teenagers and young people playing volleyball and football, surrounded by cheering crowds and children who played around the edges of the pitches. This time the games were much smaller and infrequent, and at dusk a strange quietness and solitude seemed to fall upon the houses—there were far fewer teenagers and young people than before.

I wondered, at first, whether this was just my own impression or some sense of the melancholia that is well known to anthropologists and that famously led Claude Lévi-Strauss (1972) to call the tropics "*tristes*." Then, on my way back, I ran into Diego in the city. He has moved there permanently, and we reminisced about my first travels to the village.

DIEGO: Do you remember how you played with the children when you first came to the village?

CAMILLA: Yes, of course! It was the best time of my life.

DIEGO: Now the village is so sad, isn't it? I don't want to spend time there anymore.

CAMILLA: Really? Why?

DIEGO: It's so empty. All the young people have left. Do you remember how we used to play football every night? Now nobody does anymore. It's so empty. I was getting sad there. I don't want to live there anymore.

I met several other young people from different villages, and they all said the same thing: "the villages are sad now" and "all the youth are leaving the forest." During my earliest years of fieldwork, in 2010–2014, most people in the community where I work had seen a city only once or twice, if at all. But over the following years, I saw travel to the *chotac* world intensify and a growing number of people settling permanently in Colonia Angamos, in Iquitos, and even in Lima, the capital of Peru, which back when I started fieldwork only a couple of people in the village had ever even been to.

Most of these migrants are young people, like Diego and other girls and boys I worked with when they were children. In the book, I have shown how this generation have been craving to access *chotac* and urban lifestyle since their earliest years, maturing a desire for the *chotac* world largely by imagining it from afar, given the impossibility of reaching it physically. Now they have grown up and are no longer *bacuëbo* (children), but *caniabo*, a term that translates as "young people" and defines the age range from puberty to adulthood (approximately between one's mid-teens and early twenties), and they are finding ways to leave the forest and fulfill their goals.

Seeing this emerging process of migration, between 2016 and 2019 I started to conduct new research in both Colonia Angamos and Iquitos, with Matses *caniabo* who have moved there, which included conducting interviews, using participatory photography and photographic walks, and, more recently, the coproduction of animated films about their lives. During this time, I have learned much about the lives of young Matses migrants, the reasons why they have left the forest, and the key challenges they have been facing and continue to face in adjusting to urban lives. This final chapter follows the lives of these migrant *caniabo*, showing how their childhood yearnings for concrete, electric light, and television have led them away from the everyday lives of their parents and grandparents and into a new part of the world, where they are negotiating new challenges while trying to turn their childhood dreams into reality.

Becoming Slum Dwellers

A photograph I took in 2018 (figure 32) shows Diego in a park in the city, Iquitos, where locals hang out at the weekend. A few *caniabo* took me there to show me how they are starting to blend with local lifestyles and practices. Wanting to leave the village, Diego has done what a growing number of young Matses men have also chosen to do: he joined the army, which is an easy way out of the forest and one through which, perhaps, the boys can fulfill their childhood dream of becoming warriors, like their hero Jean-Claude Van Damme. Diego was proud to show me the kind of man he had become. He can speak Spanish now, he knows how to move through the city, and he also *looks* different, more like an urban youth than a forest dweller. The photograph shows him wearing a brand-new T-shirt and a sports jumper, with a fancy haircut and a pair of earbuds around his neck, which he uses to listen to music and watch videos on his secondhand smartphone (but only when he has enough money to buy internet

FIGURE 32 Diego in the city (photograph by the author).

data). He told me proudly that he sometimes goes dancing, that he has made *chotac* friends, and that he eats urban food.

When I asked Diego and other *caniabo* why they have migrated, they gave me similar answers. They said they wanted to make money and buy things for themselves, as they had been telling me since their childhood years, but they also wanted to "learn new things" and discover what city life is truly like. Scholars of migration stress that when rural people migrate to urban settings, they never do it solely for economic reasons, such as accessing waged labor, but also following a wish to become different kinds of persons and lead more desirable kinds of lives (see Collins 2018). For young Matses, this is a desire of growing up as different adults compared with their parents, and of developing new types of knowledge and skills, as visually epitomized by the photograph of Diego looking like an urban youth. This wish has begun from their earliest years, showing that for Amazonian forest dwellers and especially those who, like the Matses, live very far from cities, "urbanization often begins in people's minds and is mobilized through their desires" (Alexiades and Peluso 2015: 5).

I asked Diego to show me where he lives, and he and his cousin Tobias took me to the house where they are staying with Tobias's older sister and her two-year-old child—a wooden house on stilts built at a considerable distance from the city center of Iquitos, in the local slums (figure 33). Set in the middle of the rainforest, with a population of nearly half a million, Iquitos is the largest city in Peruvian Amazonia and can be reached only by river or air transport. The city developed in the nineteenth century, when European colonizers started investing in rubber extraction and trading, resulting in an Indigenous genocide and environmental disaster. The traces of this history are still visible in decadent Parisian-style buildings in the city's historical center, a part of town that is now popular with North American and European tourists attracted by Ayahuasca retreats and "jungle tourism" but is surrounded by a vast and growing slum classified by the government as a zone of extreme poverty. This is where young Matses migrants live, arriving in the city with no money and no resources to occupy the geographical, social, and economic periphery of the urban world.

Indeed, when they reach the city, young Matses face a series of critical challenges they had not anticipated. Most of them recount that as soon as they arrived in Iquitos for the first time, they felt overwhelmed by a feeling of *dacuëden*, the same term that children used so often when describing to me their feelings of being scared about the forest and that their parents and grandparents used to describe their terrifying encounters with spirits and forest predators. All the migrant *caniabo* I have spoken with used it to address the fear they felt when they first arrived in the world of concrete and had to learn to move amid urban traffic and *chotac* people. They recall this as a kind of shock: upon reaching the concrete land of their dreams, which they had built in their imaginations through desire, fascination, and charm during their childhood, they met a very different reality.

Wilfred, a twenty-one-year-old who is in the army with Diego, said, "Nobody had told me what a traffic light was! I didn't understand it. What's that light for?, I thought. It took me a while to figure it out." Another of these migrants is Sabrina, a twenty-six-year-old young woman who is studying to become a schoolteacher, supported by her father, who already works as one. She recounts that when she moved to Iquitos, she could not cross the street and would stand on the pavement for a long time, unsure of what to do and worried she would get run over by cars. The *caniabo* have learned how to move in the city and laughed when telling me these stories, but they nevertheless recall their initial distress and anxiety around urban traffic.

For many of these young migrants, the feeling of *dacuëden* continued as they tried to access a job, which they struggled to do given their lack of resources, their limited connections in the city, and their poor knowledge of Spanish. Many

FIGURE 33 The slums in Iquitos (photographs by Diego, twelve years old, and Nancy, fifteen).

told me about the hunger that kept them awake at night when they could not find a job and had no money to buy food. They recall walking around Mercado Belén, the main street market in Iquitos, and looking at the food stands displaying animals that in the forest people hunt during the day, or fruit that grows on their farms but is sold in the market at unaffordable prices. Most of these migrants take part in the informal economy, which in some cases means washing dishes in restaurants or cleaning hotel rooms, and in others, accessing dangerous and illegal activities—as recounted by Casey, a twenty-four-year-old migrant who grew up in a neighboring village to the one where I work: "I didn't speak Spanish at all when I moved here. I had never been to the city. Nobody would give me a job and I had no money. I became desperate. Then I started working as a security guard. It's the only job I could get. *Gracias a Diós*, nothing happened to me on the job. I left it as soon as I could."

A job as a security guard for banks or stores that hold money or goods on the outskirts of town is low-paid and comes with the awareness that people can die while doing it. A few months before Casey took on this job, a young Matses man working as a security guard was shot and killed during a robbery. While aware of this, young men have limited options, and risky or illegal jobs are often the only available choice for them to stay in the city.

Girls in the Urban World

The percentage of young women who migrate is significantly lower compared with men, partly because men are seen as money-makers and, therefore, more inclined to spend time in town to try to access waged jobs. However, in recent years a growing number of women have also started leaving the forest to try to make money themselves. Among them is Nancy, the teenage girl from the village where I worked who was part of a trip to Añushiyacu, the hunting settlement built in the middle of the forest, together with Diego. Wanting to make money and buy clothes for herself, Nancy migrated to Iquitos, where she started working washing dishes in a restaurant until she married a local *chotac* man, as so many girls aspire to do.

Nancy told me that her husband provides for her and treats her kindly, but she considers herself lucky. Many other young women have struggled to get by in the city and started selling sex, and as the *caniabo* themselves told me, sexually transmitted illnesses are spreading rapidly among them, as they are among Indigenous people all across Amazonia. A couple of years ago, news came to the village from the city that a young woman had fallen ill and was taken to the hospital. People in the village heard that she was seriously ill, and her skin was all *amarilla* (yellow). Her father flew to the city straight away, but by the time he arrived in the city and reached the hospital, he found his daughter dead. The doctors told him she died of hepatitis, an illness that he had never even heard of when he was his daughter's age and Matses people lived in the forest and had barely any contact with *chotac* people.

Several of the girls I introduced earlier in the book did not dare to go as far as Nancy and move to Iquitos, but still wanting to make money and buy clothes, they are now working as cleaners and housekeepers for local *chotac* families in Colonia Angamos. The town is easier to access for them and is perceived as a more familiar environment than Iquitos, especially because in recent years, a growing number of Matses families have built houses so that they (and their children) can spend more time there. The houses of *chotac* people are made of concrete and built in the center of town, where people must buy a lot of land from the municipality. A few Matses schoolteachers have also built their houses there, but the vast majority of Matses people cannot afford to buy lots in the center and have therefore built houses made of forest materials and set in the area surrounding the town, where the land is free. Colonia Angamos is itself classified as an area of extreme poverty by the Peruvian government, which requires special development assistance, and Matses people are building a slum area in the town, where they are becoming an even lower economic class of urban dwellers and a source of cheap labor for local *chotac*.

One of these women is Remedios, who was a teenage girl when I started working in the village and became a single mother. As we spent some time together in Colonia Angamos, Remedios took me around and showed me the town, and one evening she took me to see the house of Regina, a Matses woman from a different village who married a *chotac* shopkeeper and now lives with him and their two children in a concrete house right in the center of town. We stood outside a large open window in the house, looking in on a room where Regina was folding all her nice clothes and putting them on shelves while her two children watched television. Her husband was there and, upon noticing me, he started a conversation about his successful shop, explaining that he is a good husband and not like most men, who are always drunk and violent to their wives. As he went on talking, Remedios kept whispering to me, "Look how many clothes she's got! They are all new," and "Look how beautiful her house is."

All Matses girls know who Regina is and describe her as an ideal of success, having the kind of life to which Remedios and other migrant girls aspire. But Regina is an exceptional case, and most of the other women who have left the forest—including many of those I worked and played with during my first years of fieldwork, when they were children—have different stories to tell. When they moved to the town or the city, they had relationships with *chotac* men who would buy gifts for them, such as clothes and makeup, and took them to the *pollería*, a popular type of restaurant where the main dish is grilled chicken with fried plantain, an absolute luxury for Matses people and one of the great attractions of town. Nearly every girl I spoke with told me that same story: they were very much in love with these charming men, who promised to marry them and provide for them. But as soon as the girls became pregnant these men vanished, and in many cases the girls were unable to reach them and never heard from them again. In some cases, the girls found out that these men were already married and had families in different parts of Peru.

Remedios has a similar story. Already having a child with her cross-cousin, who left her for a *chotac* woman, she then had a second child with a *chotac* man in town, who took off shortly after the child was born and never contacted her again. When I met her in Colonia Angamos, Remedios was alone: both of her children are in the village, where her elderly parents are looking after them so she can go back to town and try to find work. When I returned to the village in 2019, I saw several elderly couples tending small children and babies: their grandchildren, left behind in the village by daughters who, like Remedios, could not afford to continue living in town with babies to provide for.

This is an unprecedented phenomenon in Matses society: as I explained, Matses women, even those from younger generations, find a sense of fulfillment in motherhood, openly saying that being a woman starts when one has children. I described how children would make fun of Paco, a boy left by his mother in the village, precisely because his was an isolated case, and a woman leaving a child behind was seen as an exceptional and out-of-the-ordinary event. But now, a growing number of young of women are leaving their children in the forest and spending time in the city, which would have been unthinkable when the now-elderly people were themselves young.

Urban Life and Its Unforeseen Perils

In 2018, I started coproducing animated films with a group of migrant *caniabo* in Iquitos centered on their lives and journeys (see Morelli 2021).[1] During our project, the young people I worked with came up with their own theories and explanation as to why they have migrated and reflected on the reasons behind the challenges they face in the city, stressing their general lack of preparation for urban life. José Antonio, twenty-three years old, pointed out that children in the villages are told little about how to behave in urban settings: "Greeting people is not part of our culture. You know, we don't do that. Before I moved to the city, the schoolteacher in my village told me that *chotac* people greet each other, saying 'hi' and 'goodbye.' So, when I arrived in Iquitos, I went to the main square. I stood there for a while and whenever someone walked by, I looked at them and said, 'Hello! Good morning!' People must have thought, 'Who is this mad guy?'" [he laughs].

While this is a funny anecdote, about which José Antonio can now laugh, the unreadiness for urban life carries much graver implications for young Matses and leaves them vulnerable to the challenges and perils of the concrete world. Wilfred, twenty-one years old, said, "In the village, we hear that people in the city party and have fun, and we have an imagination of what life there will be like. But then, when we actually get to the city, it's difficult. Young Matses think that it's easy living here. We think it's easy to get a job. But it's not. It's really hard."

Like the children I worked with, Wilfred fantasized about city life in his childhood years, and this dreaming led him to leave the forest and settle permanently in Iquitos, but he himself admits that his ideas of what city life would be like were very much based on dreamy preconceptions. After all, Matses children and youth have no opportunity to learn in the villages about urban life and its dangers. I have described how their elders show little if any interest in talking about the city, let alone spending time there, and have neither inclination nor expertise to teach their children about it. While the parents of the *caniabo* had warned them about how to avoid snakebites, jaguars, and forest spirits since they were very young, they never discussed the hazards and threats of urban settings, where most of them had barely been—after all, how could they have done so?

This lack of education toward city life was eloquently theorized by Miguel, a twenty-five-year-old Matses migrant:

> When young people leave their villages in the rainforest, they don't know what city life is like. They just don't know. In the villages, we know how to live. But here, we don't. It's a different way of living. For example, I have been living in the city for eight years. I left the forest when I was seventeen years old. In the village, I lived in a house with my family. But when I moved here, I didn't know anyone, and I had to get used to living in a room in a shared house, where I couldn't speak with anyone. I felt lonely. It's tough.

The issue of feeling lonely emerged in most of the discussions with the *caniabo* about their experiences of migrating. When they arrive in the city, young Matses usually have a few connections there, with other young people who have already migrated, but these connections are very few and dispersed, and the shift from life in the forest villages to being in the city feels drastic. I have shown that in the villages people spend most of their time together and in close proximity to one another, walking into each other's house whenever they please, and they generally dislike being alone. In the city, the *caniabo* encounter a kind of solitude they have never experienced before, for as Miguel points out, here they live with and are surrounded by strangers, which all too often leads to a sense of being radically *other* and outcasts.

Becoming *Mayu*: Social Exclusion in the City

Besides the material and economic difficulties I have described so far, another key challenge for young Matses in the city is a growing sense of social exclusion and a feeling that, as they say, *"en la ciudad, te discriminan"*: in the city, they are discriminated against by the *chotac*, something that Miguel describes in the anecdote below.

> When I finally managed to save some money, I went out to the *pollería*. I was so excited! I'd never been to a restaurant before. I sat down and ordered *pollo con platano* [chicken with fried plantains]. It's really expensive, you know: eighteen soles for the whole meal [about five US dollars]. When they brought it to me, it looked so good. It looked delicious, really. I started eating, and I was eating with my hands, I mean, all Mates people

eat with their hands. You've seen how we eat in the villages. I wasn't used to eating with knives and forks! And then I noticed the family sitting at the table next to mine. They were all staring at me—they looked at me *como si le estaba faltando de respeto* [as if I was insulting them]. I felt so embarrassed, I wanted to disappear. I didn't eat my chicken in the end. I paid, and I left.

The everyday discrimination discussed by the *caniabo* can be seen as part of a "structural racism of the state" in Peru (De La Cadena 2008: 343), where, as Peruvian anthropologists have pointed out, discrimination against Indigenous people is not only found in the public sphere but embedded in neoliberal state policies that continue to view indigeneity as an obstacle to notions of social progress and economic development (Ames 2011; Espinosa 2009; Sarmiento Barletti 2021). When I spent time with Matses people in Iquitos or Colonia Angamos, the local *chotac* would often greet me but ignore them or address them in the third person in their presence, as if they couldn't understand. "We do things differently, and the *chotac* laugh at you and point their fingers at you," the *caniabo* said, adding that this makes them feel like *mayu*—a Matses term that originally referred to other groups of Amazonian forest dwellers other than Matses but that can also have a deeply derogatory connotation, translating as "uncivilized" or "savage." During my fieldwork, I often heard young Matses men complain that local women in the city snub them—for example, they refuse to date Indigenous men or dance with them when they go clubbing—and that making friends with *chotac* people is hard because "they don't want to hang out with us."

The sense of being *mayu* was often manifest when I walked with young Matses in the town or city. I have described Matses children (and people) as being tremendously athletic, dynamic, and agile, able to swim against the Amazon currents or climb to the top of a branchless tree within seconds, to run on unstable logs used as bridges on rainforest paths, and to stand steadily on the thin gunwale of a moving canoe. But they would show none of this agility in town, often moving slowly and assuming an awkward, almost unbalanced posture not only when walking but even when standing. As we strolled on the concrete pavements I had heard them praise so much when they were children, I often found myself ahead of them, having to turn back to prompt them to speed up, and I would see them hesitating and proceeding slowly and clumsily. They would often show a sense of unease and bodily discomfort when interacting with the *chotac*, standing slantwise and at a distance from the person they were talking to while trying to avoid eye contact and often speaking with a trembling voice, indicating an embodied sense of embarrassment and inadequacy that makes them self-conscious before urban people.

When I was spending time with Remedios and the other girls in Colonia Angamos, I often watched them play volleyball in the evening. Matses girls would form a team and play against local *chotac* women, and almost every time they would lose the game. What I found striking is that Matses girls are terrific volleyball players, as I witnessed every day during my fieldwork in the forest village. But when they played in Colonia Angamos, they seemed much less agile and skilled, including Remedios herself, who was by far one the best players at home. "The *chotac* are so much better than us at volleyball" she once told me after losing a game in Colonia Angamos, but having watched them play in both places, I felt confident this was not the case. Rather, it seemed to me that in town, Matses girls lose their ability to play—yet another manifestation of their perceived sense of their own *mayu*-ness.

The *caniabo* told me that part of this sense of embarrassment and exclusion was determined by their inability to speak Spanish properly when they arrived in the city, with their lack of linguistic skills leading to a feeling of being cut out from social interactions but also of feeling scared and embarrassed, as Diego told me: "Sometimes your peers don't want to talk with you and they make fun of us, because we don't speak Spanish well. I was shy at first, and I didn't make any friends for a while. I was *natiec*."

Earlier I described being *natiec* as the feeling of being paralyzed with embarrassment, as when children lose a wordfight or are not able to stand up for themselves against the verbal attacks of another child. Diego was once the most *cuididi* or "mischievous boy" in the village, always getting the final word in verbal confrontations, and never feared wordfighting children or adults. But when he moved to the *chotac* world, he turned into a shy, *natiec* young man lacking the linguistic tools to have successful social interactions. As Sabrina put it, "In the schools at home, in the village, all the teachers are Matses. They try to teach us some Spanish, but it's very basic. They should teach us much better, because when we come here in the city, we can't speak very well. Only a few words. And that's really hard. You can't get a job, and you can't make friends."

Many young migrants are learning to see Matses as a "useless language," stressing that Matses children should learn Spanish in the village schools. The loss of native languages is experienced as a troublesome or even traumatic issue in a growing number of Indigenous societies in Amazonia and across the world, where only the elderly can still speak them fluently (Valenzuela 2012). Matses people's limited contact with the outside, the remote locations of their villages, and the fact that schoolteachers in the villages are Matses themselves and thus teach in their native language have so far contributed to preventing such language loss; but instead of seeing this as a precious resource, young Matses wish to be fluent in Spanish, and they see the language barriers they encounter in town as a major impediment. For them, these barriers feed into a sense of lacking recognition, of being unheard and unseen both by the state and by the rest of society. As Miguel said, "Sometimes I walk around with my cousin here in Iquitos, and the locals hear us speak Matses and ask, 'Hey, what's that language you're speaking? Is that English?' And when I say it's Matses, they shrug. They've never heard of it before." Even in Iquitos, the capital city of the Loreto region, where the traditional Matses territory is located, people have no idea that nearby, in the very same part of the country, lives a large population named Matses. The *caniabo* feel that not only their struggle but their very existence goes unnoticed by the wider society on whose margins they live.

Despite these difficulties, the number of young people leaving their forest villages and migrating to town and the city continues to grow. And while struggling with lack of money and living in a tiny house in the slums, Diego, Nancy, Sabrina, and the other young people who migrated are proud of the new skills they have developed and of being able to access the goods and opportunities that are only available in town and in the city. Living these different lifestyles seems to make all the troubles of urban life worth dealing with.

I have asked the *caniabo* whether they will move back to the villages one day. Diego replied with a quick and firm "no," adding, "What could I possibly do there? There's nothing to do." Nancy said the same: "What can we do in the villages? You can't work, you can't make money, there's no electricity—there's nothing to do." Other migrant *caniabo* expressed the same thought: *there's nothing in the villages*. The contrast with their own parents who grew up in deep rainforest could not be starker; for them, the forest is the center of the world, and being there is *all* one can desire. Earlier in the book I wrote about our hunting trip to Añushiyacu, where meat is still abundant and the elders spend days at a time to hunt, living like in the old days before contact. I described how Diego and Nancy, both in their early teens at the time, joined the trip and spent the whole time complaining they felt bored and kept mentioning that there is nothing to do in Añushiyacu. They could not play volleyball or football, and Diego kept asking why I hadn't brought my laptop with me to provide some sort of entertainment, which created a visible contrast with their parents, who were filled with adrenaline and kept hunting and fishing until late at night; indeed, I had never seen the elders so thrilled and excited. When I met them in the city, the *caniabo* were talking about the villages in the same way as Añushiyacu: a place devoid of opportunities, empty and now depopulated, where there is nothing to do, and where none of them envisage going back to in the future.

This process of migration will have serious implications for Matses society and for the future of Amazonia, where unprecedented numbers of people are leaving forest and rural areas to settle in towns and cities (Peluso 2015). José Antonio once told me, "in twenty years, nobody will be left in the forest." I asked him whether he truly thinks this will be the case, and he shrugged and replied, "It might be." While this is perhaps an exaggeration, the effects of young people's choice to move away are already tangible; and given the exceptionally young demographics of the Matses and other forest-dwelling groups in Amazonia and beyond, this exodus of youth will significantly transform the forest. The change is likely to happen swiftly, and within the course of one or two generations, Matses villages might look entirely different.

The Right to Self-Representation

Some of the young Matses people I work with have already spent a few years in the city, and while they still struggle with financial instability and social exclusion, they have also learned how to move among urban traffic, have become fluent in Spanish, and feel more confident when dealing with *chotac* people. A few of them have even received scholarships from the government to study at the local university (although they still need to find casual jobs to live), and two of them chose to study anthropology—including Roldán, who wrote the foreword and the afterword to this book. It seems that after all the difficulties they have encountered, their craving for *chotac* lifestyles is finally being fulfilled. But as they started becoming familiar with urban life, a new issue arose, as Roldán recalls: "Last year, I met a reporter from a local newspaper. He told me that I don't look Indigenous, that I can't possibly be Indigenous, because I'm wearing trainers and long trousers. He said that's not what Indigenous people look like. But I *am* Indigenous, of course!"

Many other *caniabo* told me similar things: the effort to chase their urban dreams has led them away from the lifestyle of their elders and the forest world, and their indigeneity is now questioned. This sense of displacement is known to affect Indigenous youth globally, leading to serious mental health issues and a rising number of youth suicides across Amazonia and worldwide (Barker et al. 2017; Virtanen 2010: 162). Working with young Manchineri in urban Brazil, Pirjo Virtanen has reported that the "folklorization of indigenous cultures" (2010: 164) in the media traps these young people in a liminal space where they no longer feel the right to claim their Indigenous belonging but nevertheless struggle to integrate into urban life.

Likewise, the *caniabo* wear trainers and listen to music on their smartphones when they can afford to buy internet data, but their desire to become new kinds of persons has turned them into what Mary Douglas called "matter out of place" (2002 [1966]: 44), trapped between the fabricated and discriminatory categories of the uncivilized savage on one side and the dangerous slum-dweller on the other. On the one hand, these Indigenous youth are seen as lower-class outsiders who do not belong or fit into the city, as shown by the family staring at Miguel in the restaurant or the girls who refuse to dance with Indigenous men; but on the other hand, they have lost the exotic charm of their grandparents and, looking more like average urban poor than nomadic forest hunters, their very indigeneity is in question, adding yet another layer to the feeling of being invisible and denied the right to self-representation.

This attitude is widely shared by reporters, tourists, and nongovernmental organizations, and in a sense even by many anthropologists, who continue to focus on how local traditional practices and worldviews are reproduced by Indigenous people in Amazonia, while paying limited if any attention to how children and youth are radically transforming these. Indeed, research with Indigenous youth in rural-to-urban transition remains extremely limited (Bird-Naytowhow et al. 2017: 1–2; Goodman et al. 2018: 315), with few ethnographic studies conducted in Amazonia (Steele 2018; Virtanen 2010, 2012), even though scholars stress that "rural-urban internal migration is perhaps one of the most pressing issues affecting indigenous peoples around the world today" (Trujano 2008: 24).

Perhaps this lack of attention to young generations of Amazonians is because their chosen lifestyles and interests lead away from the world of spirits, forest creatures, and traditional cosmologies that so captivates travelers and scholars alike. But young Matses people are making their own new choices and starting to claim their right to do so. Miguel once said this himself in a passionate speech on the matter: "Some people see you and think that because you wear clothes and trainers, you are not Indigenous. They think that if you are Indigenous, you can't leave the forest and live in the city. But being Indigenous has nothing to do with what you wear, or where you live! It's not in your clothes. It's in your heart, and it's in your way of thinking. Our culture is not static, you know; our culture is always changing. We all want to learn new things. We all have the right to change!"

While their experiences remain overlooked and their struggles go unnoticed, Matses children and young people are committed to building a new future for themselves where they continue to navigate the political, social, and economic constraints of the present in order to attain the adulthoods they desire.

Conclusion

Forest-dwelling and Indigenous people are facing unprecedented challenges not just in Amazonia but worldwide, with both their environments and cultural worldviews under critical threat. With spreading forest fires and unsustainable resource extraction, Indigenous youth suicides on the rise globally, and recent warnings that half of all Indigenous languages will be forgotten by next century (World Bank Group 2015: 27), the future of their societies looks precarious. Academic and public debate about these issues is urgent, with both Indigenous and non-Indigenous scholars stressing the global significance of indigeneity (Canessa 2018; Cepek 2018; Sillitoe 2016; Sissons 2005; Supernant 2020).

In this book, I have shown that in order to fully understand how these broad processes of change are taking place and shaping the future of Amazonia and of other regions of the world, it is necessary to take into serious consideration the experiences and viewpoints of children. Child-centered analysis is not only crucial to theorize about how change is happening over time; it is also preliminary to any policy intervention and indeed to the very possibility of establishing a sustainable society where Indigenous children and youth can benefit from the opportunities that the wider world has to offer, rather than being cut out from them.

This requires a shift in perspective and an anthropological inquiry grounded in children and young people's own viewpoints and voices, which I sought to achieve first and foremost through the use of a participatory approach based on child-centered methodologies. I have shown that Matses children are projecting themselves toward new and uncharted horizons, insofar as the kinds of adults they want to become are in many ways radically different from their elders. They crave to grow up as money-makers rather than proficient hunters and trekkers, to become urban residents instead of forest dwellers, and to access global systems of trade instead of reproducing the local sharing economy of subsistence. The very imagination of an alternative future is affecting how children act in the present, such as leaving behind forest knowledge and practices, and directing the trajectories of social life into new channels.

Finding inspiration in the work of Margaret Mead, Allison James, Christina Toren, and others, my first years of research were based on a collaborative approach that could engage children actively as respondents, something that remains limited in works concerned with Indigenous, hunter-gatherer, and forest-based childhoods.

Throughout the years, as the children have grown up, I have sought to engage them more centrally in the process of research development and knowledge production from the very outset, and I have recently started collaborating with Indigenous artists and animators to work with young migrants from different Amazonian groups and regions. In a shared and participatory process, these young people are learning to write and produce animated films as a way to share their experiences with the world beyond their communities and raise awareness about the challenges they are facing.

Seeing how much children and youth have been enjoying this work, a group of Matses elders have recently asked us to conduct collaborative projects with them, specifically to coproduce animated films that will teach the younger generations aspects of traditional knowledge that only the elderly can still recall, including oral myths and facts about medicinal plants. I discussed throughout the book how elderly Matses would often address my own skills, such as using a laptop and digital cameras, as being not so useful compared with the ability to fish, hunt, trek, and work hard within the subsistence economy. But they also acknowledged that if children and young people are to be engaged in a conversation on their heritage, which is in many ways under threat, creative and participatory methods might be the way forward. Coming from the elders themselves, this request suggests that a new future for our discipline is indeed possible—one where anthropological thinking and ethnographic practice can be applied in a collaborative process as a useful set of skills that are beneficial for the people involved rather than for mere collection of data or extraction of information from them.

My own hope for the future is for these endeavors to be pushed even further, with a new generation of Matses researchers and thinkers leading the way. Roldán was one of the children who were dreaming about concrete and playing to be Jean-Claude Van Damme in the forest when I started working with the Matses. Like many of his peers, he later migrated to the city, where he recently graduated with a degree in anthropology, and he is now working as a research collaborator in our ongoing project, "Animating the Future" that uses animation to explore youth futures in Amazonia.[1] Roldán's own dream is to become the first Matses person to earn a doctorate and work in academia, and to one day publish his own monograph.

Claude Lévi-Strauss, the most influential anthropologist to have ever worked in Amazonia, viewed social change in the region as the disappearance of cultural worlds, filled with a sense of melancholia at the thought of traditional lifestyles that were to be lost forever. Roldán is telling us a different story, one where social change is entwined with hope. I conclude the book with Roldán's moving words, which gesture toward new horizons in anthropological research and a future built by the children of the rainforest.

AFTERWORD

I started my degree without knowing what anthropology really was and what exactly it was for. I just liked the way it sounded, and I was fascinated by it. Many students or professionals from other fields tried to dissuade me. They would ask me, "What's anthropology? Are you going to study dinosaurs?" Others would say, "Why don't you study engineering or law? Anthropologists never find any work." Even so, I have not been discouraged, because I wanted to see and find out for myself. As I began to learn about anthropology, I started to feel the discipline as truly my own and as something that helped me improve myself in many ways.

Most of all, anthropology has helped me to be stronger when facing discrimination against Indigenous people and to accept my own cultural identity. I used to be ashamed to identify myself as a Matses person in front of non-Indigenous people; I was afraid they would make fun of me and reject me. But anthropology made me understand that there is not only one group or society in the world. I understood that being Indigenous does not mean that we are inferior, but rather that each group of human society has particular knowledge, and that made me break the fear that had grown inside me. I ended up telling myself with pride that I am a Matses person. If I had chosen another degree, I don't know if I would have developed this awareness; perhaps I would have kept believing that Western people are better than us. That is why for me anthropology is so important, and I want to help other young Matses who feel intimidated or ashamed to be Indigenous to throw away the idea that we are inferior.

We know that the first anthropologists dedicated themselves to studying other people, mainly small or Indigenous communities, with the aim of knowing the customs of each people that exist in the world. Thanks to them, urban society got to know some Indigenous cultures. Normally we were always informants for the *chotac* investigators. But I am currently an anthropologist, so in the future I think that we are not only going to be informants, but that we are going to write down the knowledge that our ancestors have passed down to us. And because I am very different from them, I also want to know many things about the people of the city that I have not yet learned or understood, and I want to conduct anthropological analysis about them. In the future, I want people to read my books and find my work published on the internet. I am very passionate about anthropology.

Roldán Dunú Tumi Dësi

ACKNOWLEDGMENTS

In January 2010, when our small canoe approached the rainforest village where I would spend the following twelve months and return to every year, I couldn't anticipate how fond I would become of the people who were standing on the riverbank, watching me arrive for the first time. I will be forever grateful to the Matses for welcoming me with so much kindness, affection, trust, and generosity. Thank you for letting me into your lives, for trusting me to work with your children, for inviting me to return, and for telling me you miss me when I'm not there. I miss you too, so deeply, and I think about you every day. My heart rejoices every time I see that riverbank from the canoe, which no longer feels like approaching a foreign land but like returning to a familiar place where I feel at home. My deepest affection and heartfelt gratitude is for the children this book is written about, who have brought an endless amount of joy and laughter into my life. You are always in my thoughts, children, and will be forever in my heart— *Matsesën bacuëbo, mibi tantiaquiembi*!

Some of the people in the village deserve a special mention, because without them, none of my fieldwork would have been possible. My whole research could only take place thanks to Daniel Jimenez and his wonderful wife, Mercid Ushiñahua, who bestowed absolute trust on me from the moment they invited me to live in their community. Gracias, Daniel y Mercid, los quiero mucho y siempre pienso en ustedes. My life in the village (and outside) would not be the same without some of the people whom I now love like my own family, and who always take care of me like I am theirs—Cesar and Veronica, Lucho and Marina, Delicia, Liliana, Franscisca, Aurora, Dana, Aurelia, and Patricia. I am especially grateful to my dearest friend, Cindy Jimenez, whom I have seen grow from a cool teenage girl into a beautiful Amazonian woman and an amazing mother. (Cindy, remember the day you took me fishing, when I had just arrived in the village and didn't know anyone, and we laughed for hours, without actually catching any fish? It was one of best days of my life, and you are one of the people I love the most in this world.) I am much indebted to Roldán Dunú Tumi Dësi, the very first Matses to graduate in anthropology, who wrote the foreword and afterword to this book. I am so proud to be working with you, Roldán, and I look forward to reading your own book, which will change the horizons of a discipline that must be honored to have you in it.

This book is partly based on my doctoral research, which was carried out and funded by the Department of Anthropology at the University of Manchester. I became interested in doing research in Amazonia during my undergraduate degree at La Sapienza, University of Rome, when I read a paper written by Paul Henley, and I felt so privileged to become his student at Manchester. Grazie mille, Paul, for introducing me to Amazonia and sharing your passion with me. I am so grateful to Gillian Evans, my thesis co-supervisor, for pushing me to think about childhood outside of standard preconceptions, as well as to Peter Wade, Michelle Obeid, Jeanette Edwards, Soumhya Venkatesan, Stef Jansen, and Michael Atkins for their precious comments and support throughout my PhD, and for making Manchester such an inspiring and stimulating research environment. I am also thankful to Mark Harris and Tony Simpson, who examined my thesis and offered kind, encouraging comments on my work.

Many people supported my research in Peru. David Fleck shared his incredible knowledge of Matses language and the forest environment; Jean-Pierre Chaumeil introduced me to Iquitos, its troubled past, and its beauty; and Guillermo Pëmen, my dear friend and collaborator, passed on to me some of his creative visions by giving me frog poison.

I wrote much of this book while working at the Department of Anthropology and Archaeology at the University of Bristol where, like in the rainforest, I quickly felt at home. I am grateful to Sarah Winkler-Reid for introducing me to Bristol, and to all the colleagues who have created such a supportive and welcoming work environment, especially Fiona Jordan, Mhairi Gibson, Graeme Were, Neil Carrier, and David Cooper. I was so fortunate to work with Alice Elliot, a truly incredible scholar and woman, whose powerful words of encouragement have much strengthened my confidence in myself and my work. Many of the ideas in this book have taken shape through conversations I had with my dear friends and colleagues Amy Penfield and Juan Zhang, who every day show me how women can fully, unreservedly support each other at work and in life. You are an inspiration, Juan and Amy, and Bristol is an infinitely better place with you in it.

I could only ever follow the path that led me to write this book, starting with the rather unusual choice of conducting anthropological research, because I was blessed with a family who have always backed me with all their means. My parents, Alessandro and Paola, have supported me with unconditional love and trust even when I took roads that seemed incomprehensible; from when they let me free to roam the Tuscan woods as a child, to when they drove me in tears to an airport as I was about to disappear for months into a much bigger forest. My adored sister, Carlotta, has listened so many times to my stories about the forest as much as the Matses have heard about her. She never got tired of asking me questions, much like they never got tired of asking, "When are you bringing her here?" Grazie, vi voglio tutto il bene del mondo.

I am delighted that my book is being published in the Rutgers Series in Childhood Studies, and I have thoroughly enjoyed working with the marvelous editorial team. I am deeply thankful to Kimberly Guinta for being so encouraging from the very start; to Jasper Chang, Carah Naseem, and Vincent Nordhaus for their fantastic support throughout; and to John Donohue for his patient work. I am also grateful to the anonymous reviewers; those who loved the book, offering much needed reassurance and hope, and those who hated it, for helping me write a much better version of it. I am so thankful to Simon Lord, the best writer I know, for his wonderful comments and support.

The concluding parts of the book are based on new research funded by the British Academy, to whom I am hugely grateful, and centered on coproduction of animated films. This would have not been possible without the passionate work of my collaborator, Sophie Marsh, to whom I owe all my new research adventures in the rainforest and beyond. Sophie, thank you for working with me, for bringing happiness to Matses children with your animation magic, for listening so patiently to my convoluted anthropological thoughts, and for lending me your jacket in the cold forest nights. You are an extraordinary artist and an incredible friend.

Embarking on an academic career as a young woman in a foreign country, with no existing contacts or previous experience in British academia, has not been an easy journey. And if I was able to even consider doing so, it is only because I had the immense privilege and true blessing of meeting my mentor, Andrew Irving, who has inspired all my best research ideas and continues to be a light shining in the dark. Thank you, Andrew, for believing in that shy immigrant who knew half of the words written in this book, and will never know enough to express all of her love and gratitude for you.

SOME OF THE MATERIAL PRESENTED here previously appeared in the following publications, and I thank the editors and publishers for their permission to reprint:

"Do Forest Children Dream of Electric Light? An Exploration of Matses Children's Imaginings in Peruvian Amazonia." In *Reflections on Imagination: Human Capacity and Ethnographic Method*, edited by M. Harris and N. Rapport, 215–234. Farnham, UK: Ashgate, 2015.

"The River Echoes with Laughter: A Child-Centred Analysis of Social Change in Amazonia." *Journal of the Royal Anthropological Institute*, 23(1) (2017): 137–154.

"A View from the Ground: Using Participatory Photography with Hunter-Gatherer Children (Peru)." *AnthropoChildren* (online), issue 10 (forthcoming).

NOTES

INTRODUCTION

1. To reach Matses villages from Lima, the capital of Peru, one must take a one-hour domestic flight to Iquitos, the major city in the Loreto department, in the northern Amazonian region of Peru. Then, from Iquitos, another one-hour flight operated by the Peruvian military reaches Colonia Angamos, the seat of the Yaquerana district and the closest *chotac* settlement to Matses territory. From Colonia Angamos, Matses villages are reached by motorized canoes—it takes between eight and twelve hours to reach the village where I have conducted most of my fieldwork.

2. Anthropologist Steven Romanoff conducted research with the Matses in the 1970s and recorded a number of five hundred people, while linguist David Fleck, working in the 1990s, recorded over two thousand, and the number is growing. This shows a dramatic demographic boom that has taken place following sedentary life, meaning that the current Matses population is now extremely young.

3. For the first few weeks, I conducted interviews with both children and adults with the help of Enrique, the village chief, who helped me translate into Spanish; after a couple of months I started feeling comfortable having basic everyday interactions and conversations, and after six months I was able to conduct full-length interviews by myself.

CHAPTER 1   THE CHILD IN THE FOREST

1. Besides its use as an ethnonym and a noun meaning "person" or "people," the term is also used as an adjective, for example, in the phrase "Matses lifestyle and practices," and to refer to the language spoken by Matses people, which is part of the Panoan linguistic family.

CHAPTER 3   THE SOUND OF INEQUALITY

1. Some analytical examples of children's role as active economic agents and their relations with monetary practice are offered by Deborah Levison (2000), Heather Montgomery (2007), and Aviva Sinervo (2013).

CHAPTER 4   CONSUELO'S DOLLS

1. In this chapter I focus on girls and women, and in chapter 5 on boys and men. An analysis of gender based on a distinction between "women" and "men" will appear heteronormative to a Western audience, but it very much reflects a dichotomous view of gender shared by the Matses and other Amazonian groups. Indeed, in Matses and

other forest-dwelling Amazonian societies, this distinction—and the interaction between adult women and men—forms the very basis of the household economy and social structures, as I discuss in the chapter.

2. The Matses terms I am translating as "cross-cousins" are *mëntado* (male cross-cousin) and *shanu* (female cross-cousin), but it is vital to note that a Matses person would never address them as "cousin": the words sound more like "boyfriend" or "girlfriend," or "lover." So, when Lorena asks me how many *shanu* my father has—although *shanu* literally addresses the offspring of his dad's sisters or his mother's brothers—she actually means girlfriends or lovers, in other words, women who have sexual intercourse with him without being married. If a Matses man has sexual intercourse with a *chotac* woman, he can thereafter call her his *shanu*, literally his cross-cousin but meaning his lover. The equivalent for women is *mëntado*, which translates as "male cross-cousin" but also as "lover" or "boyfriend."

3. Blanca Muratorio (1998) highlighted similar intergenerational clashes in her work with Napo Quichua women in Ecuador, where young women in rural communities are particularly vulnerable to the charms of urban practices, such as using makeup, dancing in nightclubs, watching television, and having sex with non-Indigenous men. Elderly women are vocally critical of this behavior, which they see as harmful and against traditional values of Quichua womanhood. Elderly Matses women do not complain about girls craving *chotac* lifestyles with the same intensity, but the older generations do see their lack of *dayac*-ness as being less "womanly" compared with how women from older generations used to be.

CHAPTER 5   JEAN-CLAUDE VAN DAMME IN THE RAINFOREST

1. Classic child-centered accounts on peer-group dynamics include the work of William Corsaro (1997, 2003), Marjorie Goodwin (2006), Allison James (1993, 1998), and Barrie Thorne (1993). See also Amy Kyratzis (2004) for a review.

2. While the very definition of "peer group" can be problematic, here I use the term to address the group of children from the age of five or six to about thirteen, who spend much time every day playing together. As is common to hunter-gatherer societies, Matses children in this age range often spend time together without splitting into smaller groups according to age and gender, even though, occasionally, boys and girls play separately.

CHAPTER 7   URBAN FUTURES

1. While animation has not been applied much in anthropological research, a number of academic researchers have been coproducing animated films with Huichol children in Mexico (Davenport and Gunn 2009) and video games with Huni Kuin people in Amazonia, inspired by their mythology (Meneses 2017)—seeking to merge digital illustration techniques and Indigenous narratives, art, and aesthetics.

CONCLUSION

1. The project is based at the University of Bristol and conducted in partnership with the Pontificia Universidad Católica del Perú, and it is funded by the British Academy.

REFERENCES

Aikman, S. (1996). "Interculturality and Intercultural Education: A Challenge for Democracy." *International Review of Education*, 43(5–6): 463–479.

Aikman, S. (2002). "Women's Oral Knowledge and the Poverty of Formal Education in the SE Peruvian Amazon." *Gender and Development*, 10(3): 41–50.

Alexiades, M. N. (2009). *Mobility and Migration in Indigenous Amazonia: Contemporary Ethnoecological Perspectives*. New York: Berghahn Books.

Alexiades, M. N., and D. M. Peluso. (2015). "Introduction: Indigenous Urbanization in Lowland South America." *Journal of Latin American and Caribbean Anthropology*, 20: 1–12.

Allerton. C., ed. (2016). *Children: Ethnographic Encounters*. London: Bloomsbury.

Ames, P. (2011). "Cultura y desigualdad: Discriminación, territorio y jerarquías en redefinición." *Balances Críticos*. Lima: Instituto de Estudios Peruanos, 225–271.

Ames, P. (2021). "Educación, ¿La mejor herencia o el mejor negocio? La segregación educativa en el Perú y los desafíos para la ciudadanía democrática." *Revista Peruana de Investigación Educativa*, 1: 9–36.

Anderson-Levitt, K. M. (2005). "The Schoolyard Gate: Schooling and Childhood in Global Perspective." *Journal of Social History*, 38(4): 987–1006.

Århem, K. (1996). "The Cosmic Food Web: Human-Nature Relatedness in the Northwest Amazon." In *Nature and Society: Anthropological Perspectives*, edited by P. Descola and G. Pálsson, 185–204. London: Routledge.

Austin, J. L. (1962). *How to Do Things with Words*. Oxford: Clarendon Press.

Barker, B., A. Goodman, and K. DeBeck. (2017). "Reclaiming Indigenous Identities." *Canadian Journal of Public Health*, 108(2): 208–210.

Bird-David, N. (1990). "The Giving Environment: Another Perspective on the Economic System of Gatherer-Hunters." *Current Anthropology*, 31(2): 189–196.

Bird-David, N. (1992). "Beyond 'The Hunting and Gathering Mode of Subsistence': Culture-Sensitive Observations on the Nayaka and Other Modern Hunter-Gatherers." *Man*, 27(1): 19–44.

Bird-David, N. (2005). "Studying Children in 'Hunter-Gatherer' Societies: Reflections from a Nayaka Perspective." In *Hunter-Gatherer Childhoods*, edited by B. S. Hewlett and E. Lamb, 92–105. New York: Aldine.

Bird-Naytowhow, K., A. R. Hatala, T. Pearl, A. Judge, and E. Sjoblom. (2017). "Ceremonies of Relationship: Engaging Urban Indigenous Youth in Community-Based Research." *International Journal of Qualitative Methods*, 16: 1–14.

Blackwell, M. (2012). "The Practice of Autonomy in the Age of Neoliberalism: Strategies from Indigenous Women's Organising in Mexico." *Journal of Latin American Studies*, 44(4): 703–732.

Bloch, M. (2012). *Anthropology and the Cognitive Challenge*. Cambridge: Cambridge University Press.

Bloch, M. N., and S. M. Adler. (1994). "African Children's Play and the Emergence of the Sexual Division of Labor." In *Children's Play in Diverse Cultures*, edited by J. Roopnarine, J. E. Johnson, and F. H. Hooper, 148–178. Albany: State University of New York Press.

Brant-Castellano, M. (2004). "Ethics of Aboriginal Research." *Journal of Aboriginal Health*, 1: 98–114.

Briggs, J. L. (1998). *Inuit Morality Play: The Emotional Education of a Three-Year-Old*. New Haven, CT: Yale University Press.

Butler, J. (1990). *Gender Trouble: Feminism and the Subversion of Identity*. New York: Routledge.

Canessa, A. (2018). "Indigenous Conflict in Bolivia Explored through an African Lens: Towards a Comparative Analysis of Indigeneity." *Comparative Studies in Society and History*, 60(2): 308–337.

Cepek, M. (2018). *Life in Oil: Cofán Survival in the Petroleum Fields of Amazonia*. San Antonio: University of Texas Press.

Chapin, B. (2014). *Childhood in a Sri Lankan Village: Shaping Hierarchy and Desire*. New Brunswick, NJ: Rutgers University Press.

Chaumeil, J-P. (2009). "Transformación de un sistema médico indígena: Cuerpo y cirugía entre los Yagua de la Amazonia peruana." In *Salud e interculturalidad en América Latina: Practicas quirúrgicas y pueblos originarios*, edited by G. Fernández-Juárez, 87–94. Quito: Abya Yala Publicaciones.

Chirif, A. (2017). *Después del caucho*. Lima: CAAAP.

Cohn, C. (2014). "Concepções de infância e infâncias: Um estado da arte da antropologia da criança no Brasil." *Civitas—Revista de Ciências Sociais*, 13(2): 221.

Cole, J., and D. Durham. (2008). *Figuring the Future: Globalization and Temporalities of Children and Youth*. Santa Fe, NM: School for Advanced Research Press.

Collins, F. L. (2018). "Desire as a Theory for Migration Studies: Temporality, Assemblage and Becoming in the Narratives of Migrants." *Journal of Ethnic and Migration Studies*, 44(6): 964–980.

Corsaro, W. (2003). *We're Friends, Right? Children's Use of Access Rituals in a Nursery School*. Washington, DC: Joseph Henry Press.

Corsaro, W. A. (1997). *The Sociology of Childhood*. London: Pine Forge Press.

Corsaro, W. A. (2011). "Peer Cultures." In *The Palgrave Handbook of Childhood Studies*, edited by J. Qvortrup, W. A. Corsaro, and M. S. Honig, 301–315. Basingstoke, UK: Palgrave Macmillan.

Cox, R., A. Irving, and C. Wright. (2016). "Introduction: The Sense of the Senses." In *Beyond Text? Critical Practice and Sensory Anthropology*, edited by R. Cox, A. Irving, and C. Wright, 1–19. Manchester: Manchester University Press.

Crapanzano, V. (2004). *Imaginative Horizons: An Essay in Literary-Philosophical Anthropology*. Chicago: University of Chicago Press.

Davenport, M. G., and K. Gunn. (2009). "Collaboration in Animation: Working Together to Empower Indigenous Youth." *Art Education*, 62: 6–12.

De La Cadena, M. (2008). "Alternative Indigeneities: Conceptual Proposals." *Latin American and Caribbean Ethnic Studies*, 3(3): 341–349.

De Martino, E. (1977). *La fine del Mondo: Contributo all'analisi delle apocalissi culturali*. Torino: Einaudi.

Denov, M., D. Doucet, and A. Kamara. (2012). "Engaging War Affected Youth through Photography: Photovoice with Former Child Soldiers in Sierra Leone." *Intervention*, 10: 117–133.

Descola, P. (1992). "Societies of Nature and the Nature of Society." In *Conceptualizing Society*, edited by A. Kuper, 107–126. New York: Routledge.

Descola, P. (1994). *In the Society of Nature: A Native Ecology in Amazonia.* Cambridge: Cambridge University Press.

Dhir, R. K., U. Cattaneo, M. V. Cabrera Ormaza, H. Coronado, and M. Oelz. (2019). *Implementing the ILO Indigenous and Tribal Peoples Convention No. 169: Towards an Inclusive, Sustainable and Just Future.* Geneva: International Labour Organization.

Douglas, M. (2002 [1966]). *Purity and Danger: An Analysis of Concepts of Pollution and Taboo.* London: Routledge.

Espinosa, O. (2009). "Ciudad e identidad cultural: ¿Cómo se relacionan con lo urbano los indígenas amazónicos peruanos en el siglo XXI?" *Bulletin de l'Institut français d'études andines*, 38(1): 47–59.

Ewart, E. (2007). "Black Paint, Red Paint and a Wristwatch: The Aesthetics of Modernity among the Panard in Central Brazil." In *Body Arts and Modernity*, edited by E. Ewart and M. O'Hanlon, 36–52. Wantage, Oxon, UK: Sean Kingston.

Fabian, J. 1983. *Time and the Other: How Anthropology Makes Its Object.* New York: Columbia University Press.

Feather, C. (2009). "The Restless Life of the Nahua: Shaping People and Places in the Peruvian Amazon." In *Mobility and Migration in in Indigenous Amazonia: Contemporary Ethnoecological Perspectives*, edited by M. Alexiades, 69–85. London: Berghahn Books.

Ferguson, J. (1999). *Expectations of Modernity: Myths and Meaning of Urban Life on the Zambian Copperbelt.* Berkeley: University of California Press.

Fleck, D. (2003). "A Grammar of Matses." PhD dissertation, Rice University.

Gargallo, F. (2006). *Las ideas feministas latinoamericanas.* México: UACM.

Gasché, J. (1997). "Mas allí de la cultura: Lo político. Teoría y practica de un programa de formación de maestros indígenas amazónicos de Perú." In *Indígenas en las escuela*, edited by M. Bertely Busquets and A. Robles Valle, 219–244. México: Consejo Mexicano de Investigación Educativa.

Gasché, J. (2004). "Hacia una propuesta curricular intercultural en un mundo global." *Revista Interamericana de Educación de Adultos*, 27(1): 177–200.

Gaskins, S. (2003). "From Corn to Cash: Change and Continuity within Mayan Families." *Ethos*, 31: 248–273.

Gaskins, S., and R. Paradise. (2010). "Learning through Observation in Daily Life." In *The Anthropology of Learning in Childhood*, edited by D. F. Lancy, J. C. Bock, and S. Gaskins, 85–117. Lanham, MD: AltaMira Press.

Goodman, A., M. Snyder, and K. Wilson. (2018). "Exploring Indigenous Youth Perspectives of Mobility and Social Relationships: A Photovoice Approach." *The Canadian Geographer*, 62: 314–325.

Goodwin, M. H. (2006). *The Hidden Lives of Girls: Games of Stance, Status, and Exclusion.* Oxford: Blackwell.

Guerrero, A. L., and T. Tinkler. (2010). "Refugee and Displaced Youth Negotiating Imagined and Lived Identities in a Photography-Based Educational Project in the United States and Colombia." *Anthropology and Education Quarterly*, 41(1): 55–74.

Harris, M. (2007). "Introduction: 'Ways of Knowing.'" In *Ways of Knowing: Anthropological Approaches to Crafting Experience and Knowledge*, edited by M. Harris, 1–24. Oxford: Berghahn Books.

Harrison, F. (2010a). "Anthropology as an Agent of Transformation: Introductory Comments and Queries." In *Decolonizing Anthropology: Moving Further toward an Anthropology for*

Liberation, edited by F. Harrison, 1–15. 3rd ed. Arlington, VA: American Anthropological Association.

Harrison, F. (2010b). "Ethnography as Politics." In *Decolonizing Anthropology: Moving Further toward an Anthropology for Liberation*, edited by F. Harrison, 88–110. 3rd ed. Arlington, VA: American Anthropological Association.

Heidbrink, L. (2020). *Migranthood: Youth in a New Era of Deportation*. Stanford, CA: Stanford University Press.

Heidegger, M. (1962) [1927]. *Being and Time*. Oxford: Blackwell.

High, C. (2010). "Warriors, Hunters, and Bruce Lee: Gendered Agency and the Transformation of Amazonian Masculinity." *American Ethnologist*, 37(4): 753–770.

INEI (Instituto Nacional de Estadistica e Informatica). (2007). "Censos nacionales 2007 XI de población y VI de vivienda." http://censos.inei.gob.pe/cpv2007/tabulados/#.

Ingold, T. (1987). *The Appropriation of Nature: Essays on Human Ecology and Social Relations*. Iowa City: University of Iowa Press.

Ingold, T. (1993). "The Temporality of the Landscape." *World Archaeology*, 25(2): 152–174.

Ingold, T. (2010). *Bringing Things to Life: Creative Entanglements in a World of Material*. Manchester: ESRC National Centre for Research Methods.

Irving, A. (2007). "Ethnography, Art, and Death." *Journal of the Royal Anthropological Institute*, 13: 185–208.

Irving, A. (2011). "Strange Distance: Towards an Anthropology of Interior Dialogue." *Medical Anthropology Quarterly*, 25(1): 22–44.

Jackson, M. (2013). *The Politics of Storytelling: Variations on a Theme by Hannah Arendt*. 2nd ed. Copenhagen: Museum Tusculanum Press.

James, A. (1993). *Childhood Identities: Self and Social Relationships in the Experience of the Child*. Edinburgh: Edinburgh University Press.

James, A. (1998). "Play in Childhood: An Anthropological Perspective." *Child Psychology and Psychiatric Review*, 3(3): 104–105.

James, A. (2007). "Giving Voice to Children's Voices: Practices and Problems, Pitfalls and Potentials." *American Anthropologist*, 109(2): 261–272.

James, A., and A. Prout. (1997). "Introduction." In *Constructing and Reconstructing Childhood*, edited by Allison James and Alan Prout, 1–6. 2nd ed. London: Routledge.

Kensinger, K. M. (1995). *How Real People Ought to Live: The Cashinahua of Eastern Peru*. Prospect Heights, IL: Waveland Press.

Kulick, D., and M. Willson. (1994). "Rambo's Wife Saves the Day: Subjugating the Gaze and Subverting the Narrative in a Papua New Guinea Swamp." *Visual Anthropology Review*, 10(2): 1–13.

Kullman, K. (2012). "Experiments with Moving Children and Digital Cameras." *Children's Geographies*, 10: 1–16.

Kyratzis, A. (2004). "Talk and Interaction among Children and the Co-construction of Peer Groups and Peer Culture." *Annual Review of Anthropology*, 33: 625–649.

Lagrou, E. M. (2001). "Homesickness and the Cashinahua Self: A Reflection on the Embodied Condition of Relatedness." In *The Anthropology of Love and Anger: The Aesthetics of Conviviality in Native Amazonia*, edited by J. Overing and A. Passes, 152–169. London: Routledge.

Lancy, D. F. (1996). *Playing on the Mother-Ground: Cultural Routines for Children's Development*. New York: Guilford Press.

Lancy, D. F. (2008). *The Anthropology of Childhood: Cherubs, Chattel, Changelings*. Cambridge: Cambridge University Press.

Lancy, D. F. (2010). "Children's Learning in New Settings." In *The Anthropology of Learning in Childhood*, edited by D. Lancy, J. Bock, and S. Gaskins, 443–464. Lanham, MD: AltaMira Press.

Lancy, D. F. (2012a). "Ethnographic Perspectives on Cultural Transmission/Acquisition." Paper presented at the School of Advanced Research (SAR) seminar on "Multiple Perspectives on the Evolution of Childhood," Santa Fe, NM, November 4–8.

Lancy, D. F. (2012b). "Unmasking Children's Agency." *AnthropoChildren*, 2: 1–20.

Levison, D. (2000). "Children as Economic Agents." *Feminist Economics*, 6: 125–134.

Lévi-Strauss, C. (1972). *Tristes Tropiques*. New York: Athenaeum.

Lévi-Strauss, C. (1974 [1962]). *The Savage Mind*. 2nd ed. London: Weidenfeld and Nicholson.

Londoño-Sulkin, C. (2001). "'Though It Comes as Evil, I Embrace It as Good': Social Sensibilities and the Transformation of Malignant Agency among the Muinane." In *The Anthropology of Love and Anger: The Aesthetics of Conviviality in Native Amazonia*, edited by J. Overing and A. Passes, 170–186. London: Routledge.

Maurer, B. (2006). "The Anthropology of Money." *Annual Review of Anthropology*, 35(1): 15–36.

McCallum, C. (2003). *Gender and Sociality in Amazonia: How Real People Are Made*. Oxford: Berg.

Mead, M. (1932). "An Investigation of the Thought of Primitive Children, with Special Reference to Animism." *Journal of the Royal Anthropological Institute of Great Britain and Ireland*, 62: 173–190.

Mead, M. (1977). "Children, Culture, and Edith Cobb." Paper presented at Children, Nature, and the Urban Environment: Proceedings of a Symposium-Fair, 18–24. Upper Darby, PA: U.S. Department of Agriculture, Forest Service, Northeastern Forest Experiment Station.

Mead, M. (2001) [1928]. *Coming of Age in Samoa*. Harmondsworth, UK: Penguin.

Meneses, G. G. (2017). "Pinho Meneses Saberes em Jogo: A Criação do Videogame Huni Kuin: Yube Baitana." *Gesto, Imagem e Som—Revista de Antropologia*, (2)1: 83–109.

Mezzenzana, F. (2020). "Between Will and Thought: Individualism and Social Responsiveness in Amazonian Child Rearing." *American Anthropologist*, 122: 540–553.

Mitchell, L. M. (2006). "Child-Centered? Thinking Critically about Children's Drawings as a Visual Research Method." *Visual Anthropology Review*, 22: 60–73.

Montgomery, H. (2007). "Working with Child Prostitutes in Thailand: Problems of Practice and Interpretation." *Childhood*, 14(4): 415–430.

Montgomery, H. (2009). *An Introduction to Childhood: Anthropological Perspectives on Children's Lives*. Malden, MA: Wiley-Blackwell.

Moore, H. L. (1994). *A Passion for Difference: Essays in Anthropology and Gender*. Bloomington: Indiana University Press.

Morelli, C. (2013). "Teaching in the Rainforest: Exploring Matses Children's Affective Engagement and Multisensory Experiences in the Classroom Environment." *Teaching Anthropology*, 2(2): 53–65.

Morelli, C. (2015). "Do Forest Children Dream of Electric Light? An Exploration of Matses Children's Imaginings in Peruvian Amazonia." In *Reflections on Imagination: Human Capacity and Ethnographic Method*, edited by M. Harris and N. Rapport, 215–234. Farnham, UK: Ashgate.

Morelli, C. (2017). "The River Echoes with Laughter: A Child-Centred Analysis of Social Change in Amazonia." *Journal of the Royal Anthropological Institute*, 23(1): 137–154.

Morelli, C. (2021). "The Right to Change Co-producing Ethnographic Animation with Indigenous Youth in Amazonia." *Visual Anthropology Review*, 37(2): 333–355.

Muratorio, B. (1998). "Indigenous Women's Identities and the Politics of Cultural Reproduction in the Ecuadorian Amazon." *American Anthropologist*, 100(2): 409–420.

Orellana, M. F. (2009). *Translating Childhoods: Immigrant Youth, Language, and Culture*. New Brunswick, NJ: Rutgers University Press.

Overing, J. and Passes, A. (2000). "Introduction: Conviviality and the Opening Up of Amazonian Anthropology." In *The Anthropology of Love and Anger: The Aesthetics of Conviviality in Native Amazonia*, edited by J. Overing and A. Passes, 1–31. Cambridge: Cambridge University Press.

Pandian, A. 2019. *A Possible Anthropology: Methods for Uneasy Times*. Durham, NC: Duke University Press.

Peluso, D. (2015). "Circulating between Rural and Urban Communities: Multisited Dwellings in Amazonian Frontiers." *Journal of Latin American and Caribbean Anthropology*, 20(1): 57–79.

Penfield, A. 2023. *Predatory Economies: The Sanema and the Socialist State in Contemporary Amazonia*. Austin: University of Texas Press.

Pink, S. (2011) "Images, Senses and Applications: Engaging Visual Anthropology." *Visual Anthropology*, 24(5): 437–454.

Reyes-García, V., and A. Pyhälä, eds. (2017). *Hunter Gatherers in a Changing World*. New York: Springer.

Rival, L. (1998). "Androgynous Parents and Guest Children: The Huaorani Couvade." *Journal of the Royal Anthropological Institute*, 4(4): 619–642.

Rival, L. (2002). *Trekking through History: The Huaorani of Amazonian Ecuador*. New York: Columbia University Press.

Rival, L. (2006). "Amazonian Historical Ecologies." *Journal of the Royal Anthropological Institute*, 12: 79–94.

Rivière, P. 1969. *Marriage among the Trio: A Principle of Social Organization*. Oxford: Clarendon Press.

Rockwell, E., and A. M. R. Gomes. (2009). "Introduction to the Special Issue: Rethinking Indigenous Education from a Latin American Perspective." *Anthropology and Education Quarterly*, 40(2): 97–109.

Rogoff, B., R. Paradise, R. M. Arauz, M. Correa-Chávez, and C. Angelillo. (2003). "Firsthand Learning through Intent Participation." *Annual Review of Psychology*, 54(1): 175–203.

Romanoff, S. A. (1983). "Women as Hunters among the Matses of the Peruvian Amazon." *Human Ecology*, 11(3): 339–343.

Romanoff, S. A. (1984). "Matses Adaptations in the Peruvian Amazon." PhD dissertation, Columbia University.

Salmond, A. 1982. "Theoretical Landscapes: On Cross-Cultural Conceptions of Knowledge." In *Semantic Anthropology*, edited by D. Parkin, 65–87. London: Academic Press.

Santos-Granero, F. (2009). "Hybrid Bodyscapes: A Visual History of Yanesha Patterns of Cultural Change." *Current Anthropology*, 50(4): 477–512.

Sarmiento Barletti, J. P. (2022). "Between Care and Conflict: Relations of Resource Extraction in the Peruvian Amazon." *Bulletin of Latin American Research*, 41(3): 435–449.

Segato, R. L. (2014). "El sexo y la norma: Frente estatal, patriarcado, desposesión, colonidad." *Revista Estudos Feministas*, 22(2): 304, 593.

Sempértegui, A. (2021). "Indigenous Women's Activism, Ecofeminism, and Extractivism: Partial Connections in the Ecuadorian Amazon." *Politics & Gender*, 17(1): 197–224.

Sillitoe, P. (2016). *Indigenous Studies and Engaged Anthropology: The Collaborative Moment*. London: Routledge.

Simpson, A. (2009). *Boys to Men in the Shadow of AIDS: Masculinities and HIV Risk in Zambia.* New York: Palgrave Macmillan.

Sinervo, A. (2013). "'No somos los pobrecitos': Negotiating Stigma, Identity, and Need in Constructions of Childhood Poverty in Cusco, Peru." *Childhood,* 20: 398–413.

Sissons, J. (2005). *First Peoples: Indigenous Cultures and Their Futures.* London: Reaktion Books.

Smith, L. T. (2012). *Decolonizing Methodologies: Research and Indigenous Peoples.* 2nd ed. New York: Zed Books.

Steele, D. (2018). "Higher Education and Urban Migration for Community Resilience." *Anthropology & Education Quarterly,* 49: 89–105.

Supernant, K. (2020). "Grand Challenge No. 1: Truth and Reconciliation: Archaeological Pedagogy, Indigenous Histories, and Reconciliation in Canada." *Journal of Archaeology and Education,* 4(3): 1–22.

Suzack, C., S. M. Huhndorf, J. Perreault, and J. Barman, eds. (2010). *Indigenous Women and Feminism: Politics, Activism, Culture.* Vancouver: University of British Columbia Press.

Tassinari, A. (2007). "Concepções Indígenas de infância no Brasil." *Tellus,* 7(13): 11–25.

Taussig, M. (2011). *I Swear I Saw This: Drawings in Fieldwork Notebooks, Namely My Own.* Chicago: University of Chicago Press.

Thomson, P., ed. (2008). *Doing Visual Research with Children and Young People.* Oxon, UK: Routledge.

Thorne, B. (1993). *Gender Play.* New Brunswick, NJ: Rutgers University Press.

Toren, C. (1993). "Making History: The Significance of Childhood Cognition for a Comparative Anthropology." *Man,* 28(3): 461–478.

Toren, C. (1999). *Mind, Materiality and History Essays in Fijian Ethnography.* London: Routledge.

Toren, C. (2007). "Sunday Lunch in Fiji: Continuity and Transformation in Ideas of the Household." *American Anthropologist,* 109(2): 285–295.

Trapnell, L. A. (2008). "Conocimiento y poder: Una mirada desde la educación intercultural "bilingüe." Lima: IEP, Centro de Recursos Ibterculturales.

Trapnell, L. (2009). "Entre lenguas, entre culturas: Proceso de construcción del programa FORMABIAP. Sistematización de una experiencia Perú." Lima: IEP, Centro de Recursos Ibterculturales.

Trujano C. Y. A. (2008). *Indigenous Routes: A Framework for Understanding Indigenous Migration.* Geneva: International Organization for Migration.

Ulturgasheva, O. (2012). *Narrating the Future in Siberia: Childhood, Adolescence and Autobiography among Young Eveny.* Oxford: Berghahn Books.

Uzendoski, M. (2005). *The Napo Runa of Amazonian Ecuador.* Urbana: University of Illinois Press.

Valenzuela, P. (2012). *Voces Shiwilu: 400 años de Resistencia lingüística en Jeberos.* Lima: Fondo Editorial PUCP.

Verdery, K. (1995). "Faith, Hope, and Caritas in the Land of the Pyramids, Romania 1991–1994." *Comparative Studies in Society and History,* 37(3): 623–669.

Vinente dos Santos, F. (2012). "Mulheres indígenas, movimento social e feminismo na Amazônia: Empreendendo aproximações e distanciamentos necessários." *Revista Educamazônia–Educação, Sociedade e Meio Ambiente,* 8(1): 94–104.

Virtanen, P. (2010). "Amazonian Native Youths and Notions of Indigeneity in Urban Areas." *Identities,* 17(2–3): 154–175.

Virtanen, P. (2012). *Indigenous Youth in Brazilian Amazonia: Changing Lived Worlds.* New York: Palgrave Macmillan.

Viveiros de Castro, E. (1996). "Images of Nature and Society in Amazonian Ethnology." *Annual Review of Anthropology*, 25(1): 179–200.

Viveiros de Castro, E. (1998). "Cosmological Deixis and Amerindian Perspectivism." *Journal of the Royal Anthropological Institute*, 4(3): 469–488.

Walker, H. (2013). "Wild Things: Manufacturing Desire in the Urarina Moral Economy." *Journal of Latin American and Caribbean Anthropology*, 18(1): 51–66.

Watson-Gegeo, K. A. (2001). "Fantasy and Reality: The Dialectic of Work and Play in Kwara'ae Children's Lives." *Ethos*, 29(2): 138–158.

White, A., N. Bushin, F. Carpena-Méndez, and C. Ní Laoire. (2010). "Using Visual Methodologies to Explore Contemporary Irish Childhoods." *Qualitative Research*, 10(2): 143–158.

Willerslev, R. (2007). *Soul Hunters: Hunting, Animism, and Personhood among the Siberian Yukaghirs*. Berkeley: University of California Press.

Wood, M. (2006). "Kamula Accounts of Rambo and the State of Papua New Guinea." *Oceania*, 76(1): 61–82.

World Bank Group. (2015). *Indigenous Latin America in the Twenty-First Century: The First Decade*. Washington, DC: World Bank.

Young, L., and H. Barrett. (2001). "Adapting Visual Methods: Action Research with Kampala Street Children." *Area*, 33: 141–152.

Zelizer, V. (2002). "Kids and Commerce." *Childhood*, 9: 375–396.

INDEX

ABOUT THE AUTHOR

CAMILLA MORELLI is a lecturer in social anthropology at the University of Bristol, United Kingdom.

Available titles in the Rutgers Series in Childhood Studies